The Sisterhood *folios*

IGNITE your inner
WARRIOR

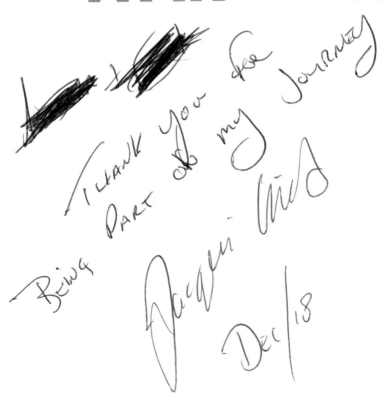

Thank you for Being Part of my Journey

Jacqui Child

Dec/18

The Sisterhood *folios*:
IGNITE YOUR INNER WARRIOR

For any information regarding permission contact
info@creativepublishinggroup.com
www.creativepublishinggroup.com

ISBN 978-1-988820-02-6

Printed in the United States of America
First publication, 2018.

Design: Amir Saarony

The Sisterhood *folios*

IGNITE your inner
WARRIOR

Creative
PUBLISHING GROUP

Acknowledgments

Lucy Ann Balzano-DeLaat

To my husband and hero, Greg, my son Tyler, parents Clara and Mike, my sister Angela, Sandy, Isabel, Lily, and Sofia. To my "M3 Soul Peeps", Kris J. and the rest who co-created my healing, believed in me, and encouraged my writing. I am because we are. I love you.

Jennifer Buttineau

To my 2 beautiful Angel babies in Heaven above ~
Olivia May and Summer Rosemary ~ You are both my inspiration and my WHY I move forward every single day. Every Breath I Breathe, I Breathe for you... Every Step I Take, I Take for You. Rest Peacefully my Angels.

To my friends, family and MOST of all my Mom and Dad, who believed in me, supported me with love and kindness every step of the way, who followed me on my journeys, ups and downs and who told me that I could do this... Well I DID IT!!
It's been a wild ride to say the least, but it's only going to be UP from here!

Jacqui Childs

My story is dedicated to my first born son, for without him I would not be here.

To my dear friend who has walked by my side without judgment. Her strength and determination to know better and do better has been truly inspirational.

My amazing husband who has risked everything to share this journey. Thanks for his love and support. I now know that I am worthy of love and respect no matter where I have been or where I'm going.

Lastly, to my youngest son who was just a boy the last time we spoke. To to him I say, be everything you think I'm not!

Laugh lots and often, I love you all.

Lucia Colangelo

To Raffaele and Apollonia, for showing us that love has no boundaries... not even heaven. And always, for my sons Jesse and Marco... you are my heartbeat. To my nieces Sabrina and Julia the most beautiful word to me next to 'Mom' is 'Zizi.'

And to my sister Giovanna aka Jova... thank you for being there for mama... you accepted her soul needed to fly when the rest of us just wanted to deny. I am truly blessed.

Lauren Dickson

I would like to thank my family, and my sweet and supportive boyfriend, for the love and laughter, which truly makes my heart smile! To God, for giving me the strength and wisdom to fight my toughest battles and embrace everything You give to me.

Sonia Dolar

I would like to dedicate this to my mother and brother.

I would like to acknowledge my family, my children and spouse, and the family I do not live with, including friends and coaches that constantly inspire me on a daily basis.

This is also written for anyone that has had the experience of being a caregiver or assitant caregiver, or will be a caregiver. May you be blessed with great strength, compassion, vision and endurance to do what you need to do.

Lots of Love, Sonia

Eileen Giudice

I would like to begin by thanking God, the Source of everything I have and the gracious builder of my faith resumé. Thank you to my parents, Ana and Angél Carrión for their endless love and support and for always being my biggest fan.

To my husband Victor, who leads our family by consistently demonstrating what unconditional love, patience, and integrity look like. The love and respect I feel for you is beyond words. Finally, to my sons, Alexander and Lucas; Thank you for helping me to experience the feeling of true selfless love. My heart is forever changed. It is my greatest honor in this life to have the privilege to be your mom. Always remember that you can do anything you set your mind to, bring kindness with you wherever you go, and never, ever give up.

Sholina Jivraj

From pain to presence to power to passion.

I could not have reached the final phase of this raw, enduring yet amazing and inspiring journey without an appreciation for the pain, the people who caused it, my own resilience and fortitude, and of course, all the healers along the way. To my beautiful daughters who remind me every single day that nothing lasts forever. To the loves who were a part of my story and always in my heart. My deepest gratitude to you all.

Resilience is brilliance, and time is not the only thing that heals all wounds.

Maimah Karmo

I want to thank God for my every blessing. I want to thank my mother and father, brothers and family for their love, care and support. I want to thank my daughter, Noelle, for being my best reflection, for choosing me as her mother, for teaching me what love really means and for being the greatest event of my life. To my friends, so much gratitude for building me up, carrying me, and for so much love, laughter and sisterhood.

I am eternally grateful that my soul exists in this human body, along with yours in this time and place. Love always, Maimah

Nikki-Monique Kurnath

With love and light, THANK YOU... God, Angels, Kurnath Family and my amazing son Dylan, relatives in Poland/Canada/US and sweet brotherhood of Stephen and Jordan. Heartfelt THANKS- supportive collegues/special friends now and then... Anna/Vicki and MDS Team, Debbie and Hypno-Healing Team, Catherine/MJ and ACOW/WE, Lori/Team LK and WBA, Carol and WLB, John and IMC, REAL Raymond, JT and IMN, Claudio and Joanne, MKM Dancers/Models, John and Cathy, and my girlz-Dana, TayTay, Heather, Kym, Ev, Sue, Ivy, my boyz-B and A, Alan, Mich, Joe, Lance, Jason, V, Marc and Blappy Nathan. Dedicated to all Single Mommies who transform into Warriors too and our Cali Fam- Lil Halen & Summer Rose.

Michelle Main

I dedicate this book to everyone and everything that has brought me to this point in my life and has helped me overcome so much.

To my amazing son Carson, you are my world and my legacy. I love you so much!

Thank you Carol Starr Taylor and Creative Publishing Group for helping make my dream of writing a book (or two) a reality. To my beautiful sisters who have contributed to this masterpiece... I love each and everyone of you.

Dr. Ingrid Pichardo Murray

I would like to thank God first and foremost for giving me the health and opportunities to be in the position that I am in today. Secondly, I want to acknowledge my family who has supported me every step of the way on this journey of self-care discovery.

Lisa Rizzo

I would like to give a special thanks to my family for supporting me in this journey as a spiritual medium. It has been a blessing to be able to walk through this life with the unconditional love of family. I wouldn't be the woman I am today if it wasn't for their support.

Carol Starr Taylor

To my beautiful children - I am so proud of the young men you have become. To the Authors in The Sisterhood Folios, past, present and future, I honor your strength, love and courage to share and inspire. To all of you, who inspire and/or teach me lessons each and everyday, I am truly grateful.

Teresa Ursini

To my darling husband Robert, who always brings out the best in me. His unconditional love and respect warms my heart and soul. My two children who have given me the privilege of being their mother. All our family and friends for their unconditional love and support. To both Dr. Franca Carella, and to Dr. Edward J. Rzadki, for all your continued help and support for our family.

Table of Contents

"It's OK if you fall down and lose your spark.
Just make sure that when you get back up,
you rise as the whole damn fire."

~ Collette Werden

Michell Smith

Foreword

We all have **Her**, the warrior hidden inside of us. Sometimes it may not feel like that. Sometimes it may feel like you are searching for **Her**, your own inner warrior, when you're facing insurmountable challenges or feeling overwhelmed. This book was written to be there for you when that might occur... to literally ignite the warrior inside of you that you seek.

She's there.

Inside these pages are stories told by warriors. Impressive stories. Stories detailing what these extraordinary women have overcome, and how they've awakened their inner warriors too. Stories that will summon **Her** in you, and serve as a reminder of how strong you really are...

They are **Her** stories.

She has served me well, my inner warrior. **She** taught me to survive.

When I was 4, a fight with my sister changed the trajectory of my life in a few breathless seconds.

As a 5-year-old, my sister pulled out all the stops to win a fight against her well matched 4-year-old adversary (me)... She told me I was adopted. She said that my parents had found me and taken me in but they no longer wanted me and were stuck with me; that they wanted to give me back, but they couldn't... and I believed her.

13

The adopted part wasn't the issue; it didn't make a big impact on its own. I looked different from my family and had already wondered the same thing, privately to myself. What devastated me was the giving me back part... the, 'I was unwanted part', the 'unlovedness'.

Now, the reality of it was that I was not adopted, I was not in danger, and there was no abuse. I won the lottery with my parents, they loved me deeply, but the power of belief is irrefutable... and I was 4.

And I believed her.

In that second, I met heartbreak... and I broke. I fell into tiny 4-year-old pieces. I never told my parents that I knew; instead I withdrew inside, and disappeared.

To survive this new reality, and the shattering of the idyllic life "before I broke", I met my inner warrior for the first time. Out of the heartbroken destruction **She** showed up to get me through.

It's a reverent experience to meet that girl; **Her**, my inner warrior. To see that look in my eyes staring back from the glass that I'd never seen before... To feel in awe of **Her** power, my power, **Her** conviction, my conviction... **She** decided we were going to be just fine, all on our own. We started saving our money so that we could move out as soon as possible... strategy in place, solution found.

I love that 4-year-old fiercely.

From that moment forward, I've never been without **Her**. **She** refused to leave me alone... We became the same.

I moved out when I was 16. I rented an apartment, signed my first lease and learned how expensive things like toilet paper and shower curtains were. Sometimes I didn't eat for a week. I was working 3 jobs while going to school and could barely make rent, so I dropped out of school for a year to work 4 jobs... Nothing was easy.

I took a psychology class my first year at university, which caused me to start questioning myself. Why did I feel the way I felt? Why was I so insecure at times? What was the logic behind why I moved out? Why was I so angry growing up?

What I knew was I'd always felt like the odd one out in my family; I was mouthy and overly assertive when I wanted something, and everything always felt like a fight. What I didn't understand was why. While I was growing up I had no idea of the impact of those two sentences that were uttered in a hot moment over a fight for the bathroom between two young children.

She had been fighting for me most of my life, and **She** was exhausted. When I ignited my inner warrior, I fed **Her** fire, and went to war every day, for years. Being fierce as a decision to keep protecting myself was no longer an acceptable, constant strategy. It kept me too sharp as an adult. I needed my warrior to mature... to learn some new moves, to figure out how to be fierce without fighting... and it was up to me to teach **Her** how.

We needed to learn how to evolve as warriors with longer fuses... to win using strategy, knowledge, strength, kindness, and performance. One who could be happy, relaxed and positive, develop relationships that allowed people in, not get thrown by negative feedback and learn to manage conflict in a better way. **She** was a fighter, a true warrior... my warrior needed a promotion. **She** needed to learn to become a Warrior Queen.

I began to study the art of war, leadership, psychology and everything self help I could find.

My love of education became channeled into understanding myself, and people. I was just 18.

Discovering the truth about that childhood argument was like finding the key to the kingdom. Telling my family about what I discovered was a surreal experience. My sister doesn't even remember the fight, and my parents never knew it happened. How powerful our words are. We must all select them carefully, especially around tiny children.

I left university and took a sales job to learn how to get better at communicating and reading people. **She** was with me when I discovered that I wasn't actually confident, that I had learned how to look confident instead... I had **Her** as I learned how to edit my beliefs and rebuild my self-esteem and self-image.

Over the next few years, we learned together, side by side my Warrior Queen in training and me, through hearing thousands of "no's" and discovering the truths to influence, leadership and possibility. **She** stuck with me when I was 21, running my first company, living in my office, sleeping on the floor behind my desk with a crowbar in the middle of an industrial park.

That was 25 years ago. Things got better. We got our promotion. The education has never stopped though; it's my favorite addiction, and source of power.

She changed my life, and has been there every time a storm arrives to get me through. We play a game together, **She** and I, naming the storms that arrive in my life alphabetically, like they do with actual tropical storms. Just to get some perspective, the last one was affectionately named Mercedes... you can do the math.

Storms will come. But we will survive, because of **Her**. **She** is in all of us, **She** is every woman.

Every woman who has ever had to look in the mirror and summon some strength from God knows where, hold her chin up and walk out the door unsure if she can pull off whatever crazy feat she takes on almost every day of her life.

She the mighty.

We are **Her** witnesses.

This is our stage.

There is no competition here.

We are all **Her**.

She is me.

She is you.

These are **Her** stories.

Best Selling Author, Consultant and Speaker, **Michell Smith** opened her first company at 21, and in 5 years scaled it to billing over 10 million dollars in annual commissions.

It was the largest and most successful sales organization ever built in Canadian history.

She's conducted over 50,000 interviews, coached thousands, helped open over 100 companies, and spoken on stage over 5000 times. It is her mission to empower women and girls to lead and succeed. She is the Founder of **She The Mighty**™ a free online school that teaches clarity, confidence, communication skills, business savvy and leadership, and has her 4th book **Dare to Lead** coming out in bookstores, Summer 2018.

Courage, above all things,
is the first quality of a warrior.
~Carl von Clausewitz

Warrior Queen

I felt a hand pressing me back, and the sensation of being in a violent centrifuge ride. The hillside violently turned into blue sky, then hillside again. Then sky. Then hill. Then blackness. But unlike in one of my film screenplays, this scene was very real. Slo... mo... and out of focus.

The crunching noise and shattering of the glass was deafening. When I came out of the blackness, smoke was billowing in my face, and I realized I was suspended. It took me a moment to realize that I was not waking from a dream. I was upside down, under the metallic weight and smell of a mangled car, hanging by my seatbelt, the only thing keeping my face from smashing into the million pebbles of glass below.

Bone rattling, the sound your windshield makes when it hits the road.

The car had rolled over twice on the icy, uninhabited country road before giving up its whirling dervish and landing on its hood. It was before the time of texting, but my inner mental chatter had caused my attention to wander from the icy conditions. I did not see the double S-bend sign, which marked the site of many fatalities.

A voice told me to turn off the car. My shaking hand reached through the dark space and switched off the ignition. The grinding noise of metal on metal (which I had not noticed until that moment) stopped, only to be replaced with an eerie silence. The only place that was not crushed inside the car was where I was floating... hanging in the false security of a surreal metal womb.

I started a body-part inventory. I noted my legs. They seemed attached. "That's good," I weighed in with all authority. I continued, wiggling my toes next. Then a wave of relief hit me as I remembered I had been traveling alone. Confused though, because I truly felt a sensation of someone holding me back and telling me I would be okay before the sickening rolling began. I was floating there, yet somehow not alone on that -25°C day in February 1998.

They say your life is a handful of defining moments. "My life flashed before my eyes" is a common term in a near-death experience. Mine certainly did: flashes of my happy childhood with loving parents; my wonderful husband on our wedding day; my new son resting against my heart in the hospital, gripping my finger. The pain, the laughter; I remembered it all. It was like watching the rushes on a film project I had written. Then, just as I was immersed in the plot, someone hit pause. I was staring at the frozen image of a young mother, my toddler son putting a crown of dandelions in my hair. It was the spring before my accident; it had been a late May afternoon. The grass was neon green with piercing yellow blooms. The irony of that idyllic moment (straight out of an allergy pill commercial I might have written) was that it was one where I had felt the most hopeless in my life. Looking back, I now understand that it was situational depression. Namely, relentless treachery in my personal life at the all too common hands of bitterness, jealousy, cruelty, and bullying– all the trappings of being surrounded by lower vibrational energy.

This was a time I lived an invisible life, with no voice. I had not yet learned the way of the Warrior. When I was treated abusively I internalized, and wondered what I had done 'wrong'. My husband, never the source, but aware of the unkindness, did not realize how bad it was or how it was affecting me. I did not yet have an understanding of how personality disorders, childhood trauma, or mental disorders could create bullying adults. My own childhood issues were affecting my ability to use my voice, and I did not have the self-awareness to see it. Most importantly, I did not have the understanding of the powerful relationship to Source that I have now as a woman, and a healer. I say this, as we truly all have gifts to give as healers if we are open to them, and if we choose to.

Those hard years bear no weight now. I have detached fully from the energies involved, and cut all cords where there was abuse. Suddenly, now, everything seems clearer. I understand that these were people of lower vibration, and, although they were doing their best, they would remain completely unaware of the misery they caused in the world, to themselves, and to others. Upon this breakthrough, a detached, deep compassion, and peace was gifted to me. The childhood traumas I will discuss in this chapter were also able to have closure. Ironically, it became the abuse that I had suffered in my life that forced me out of my comfort zone and laid the groundwork for an extraordinary life I could not have ever hoped to experience otherwise.

Back in the car on that fateful day, cold air was sucking out the last bit of heat from the metal womb, and snow from the night before had begun to drift in. I knew I would freeze soon. Unhooking my seatbelt, I turned sideways to avert my face as I fell onto glass. The driver's side window was compressed from the rollover, barely big enough to crawl through. Standing outside of the wreck, I looked up and saw I was at the bottom of a hill. Shock and adrenaline produced the strangest thoughts. "Gee," I mused, "I wonder if this is what aliens feel like when they crash land on earth." I immediately broke into hysterical laughter. Those who have survived such experiences know exactly what I speak of. Still having this strange sense I was not laughing alone, I felt someone was urging me to get to the top of the hill. Who was I to argue? So, I laughed, and I walked.

As I walked, cursing over my ripped $450 boots (as if that mattered), and with a good portion of windshield spatter in my hair, I noticed that my left hand was numb, and my right thumb had a two inch shard of glass stuck in it. I scolded the left hand as I ripped the glass out with my mouth. This made me giggle; thinking of a certain macho ex-army movie character that would have been proud. I packed my hand with snow, potty-mouthed like a truck driver, laughed some more, and went up my merry way to the top of the hill.

Good thing I did. The car that stopped to rescue me would have surely come down the hill and killed me. "You shouldn't have survived that," the officer later said at the scene, looking at me like I was a unicorn. "I wasn't alone," was my calm reply, a strange reply for someone as jaded as I was toward forces bigger than myself. "I guess so," he said, shifting his gaze back to the crushed piece of metal. I didn't realize it then, but I would never look at reality and events the same way. A new heightened awareness had already started to seed itself in my core beliefs. It was the moment I knew, just maybe, there was a lot more going on behind the scenes, that the production crew was bigger than I could ever see, and that Miss Lucy Ann didn't have all the answers after all.

As for countless writers and artists, Joseph Campbell's book, The Hero with a Thousand Faces, has become a major influencer in my quest for truth and inspired work. In it he describes 'The Hero's Journey', along a path of tribulation— from answering the call, to returning home with the 'Elixir'. That road, according to Campbell, is wrought with trials and tribulations as you 'Follow Your Bliss'. My journey has been no exception.

Before my 50th birthday, I would cheat death several times more, and have up close and personal contact with those who had crossed over. But that brutally cold February day at the scene of the car accident in 1998 is the right place for us to stand now, looking down at the snowy and glass-shattered wreck, and into the snow squalls that heralded the start of my own hero's journey.

The threshold had been crossed quite dramatically. Even Joseph Campbell would have been proud.

There are hundreds of paths up the mountain.
~ Hindu proverb

I was the girl with the metal roller skates, hanging upside down from the Mimosa tree in our front yard. I had a very happy childhood with my sister and parents, and life was about family and the simple things. We felt safe, and were never exposed to anything that would harm us, or make us feel unlovable. That all changed with one simple decision; my family moved.

Eleven years old is just a really hard time to become an immigrant to another country, never mind two moves in two years. While our house was to be built, we stayed in my grandparents' home in an Italian neighborhood of Toronto, where gossips peeped judgingly from behind curtains. Though they loved us to the best of their ability, as girls, we often felt alien, unwelcome, and uncomfortable. When the neighbors commented we were 'pretty' with our long hair, my grandmother waited until my mother left for the day and cut it off so we looked like boys. The physical beatings and bullying at school that followed were terrible. Perhaps she felt, in some twisted way, she was actually protecting us 'from too much attention'. I will never know. For many years later, I would be plagued with insecurity about my appearance.

Slowly, I lost my voice, confidence, and self-esteem. We were often excluded from family events. I can remember one incident where my sweet, beautiful mother had a veiled hurt look in her eyes as she told us that an upcoming beach and weekend farm trip was 'not for us'. My maternal grandparents had planned it for the 'boys' and their children. We were the daughter's children, and we did not carry the family name, so it seemed natural to them— not hurtful. I cried so hard that night, lamenting over my far away childhood friends, and the world I had lost. My own father, on the other hand, loved us all equally. This is the very reason I honor him by hyphenating my maiden name for this chapter.

My former academic performance could not withstand all the hits our close little family was being exposed to from the outside. A family illness added to the challenges, making me feel scared and powerless. It does explain why I am so protective of my family and wish to shield them so much. At the time, many teachers were often very abusive over my academic crash, not caring to understand the reasons behind it. I had gone from being at the top of my school in a gifted children's program back home, to falling between the cracks. By the time we had settled in our new home, I had been uprooted and labelled the 'new kid with the funny accent' twice. I had gone from a stable home with lots of healthy activities, to living in a house where I often personally felt unwanted. Most days I hid in my room. When we finally moved to our home in the country, it was bittersweet. I felt like I had been exiled to a wilderness. I escaped the cold world I was living in and was comforted by this new beginning. But this kid, that grew up with weekends in New York City, never having seen a cow, was suddenly living on a dirt road in a field right next to them! Needless to say, it took time to adjust. I eventually fell in love with Canada. How could you not?

When I was twelve the idea of adults as protectors was shattered even further when I was the victim of an attempted molestation. I bit him hard on his hand, enough to make him bleed and stop what he was doing before it got any further. I am so proud today that I did that! But it forever changed me. My parents had no idea. In one terrible moment this man caused years of depression, anxiety, a suspicious nature, and self-esteem issues. It has taken decades to overcome the experience. I carried this with me for so long, that even in adulthood I once saw a young girl who looked much like me at that age, and everything resurfaced. I found myself asking him, "Why did you do this to me?" I wondered how someone could so selfishly alter the course of someone else's life. There is never an excuse, but I now see it for the mental illness it was. I thank God for having positive men in my life; a wonderful loving father, and an amazing husband, knowing my son has had good role models.

Only very recently was I able to write a note that said, "I Forgive You", and toss it into a river. I watched it float away. This is a part of my life experience that I now have closure on, and I ask for that to be respected. I share it here to help those who have suffered sexual abuse understand they are not alone. I know the feelings of betrayal, and of having your self-esteem, ability to trust, and sense of being safe violated. You are never broken. I want you to know that. This is a big reason why I take up women's causes, and do the coaching from adversity to success that I do. It is also why the safe space of my tribe of women warriors is so important to me.

This life work grew from what I had to overcome, and how it shaped me. I will say it has been one hell of a rodeo, learning I would never survive in a cubicle, and later working for years in entertainment, and for creative agencies. In the end I have manifested some wonderful projects into my life, including an award-nominated feature film seen by millions in Africa and Europe. But everything I have done has been on the back of terrible ordeals that nearly broke me on several occasions.

You must, as Joseph Campbell says, "Follow your bliss." Critics will abound, many of the armchair variety. In fact, I can humorously share that "I have been tracking your antics on Facebook," was my greeting at one family party. The brighter your light shines, the worse it will get, but what other people think of you has nothing to do with you— and is not your concern. As to 'antics'? I encourage them strongly. It's the difference between 'doing life', and watching from a splintered bleacher. I guarantee you, without reservation, that within the next 90 years, you, and your critics, will not be here. DON'T WAIT.

Get dirty, run, scream, climb a damn tree in metal roller skates and hang upside down. Catch a ball or two– in between the ones that hit you in the face. Laugh when they hit you. Learn to move your head. It's why we are here, folks. It's never going to be easy, but it is worth it to use your gifts toward creating a life that is on purpose.

Nice Women vs. Women Who Warrior

I am not a nice person. Really. I'm not.

Stick with me on this: I have a dark side. And I am proud of it. I explore it daily, embrace it, and spend time walking it on a sturdy chain. I make choices with a full awareness of it. Let's talk about the tyranny of the Land of 'Nicedom', and a dude named Carl.

I have no shame or regrets, nor do I internalize the abuses of others. They made me level up in this video game for spiritual beings we call 'Life on Earth'. The Warrior always knows there is a lesson in everything, and adapts, and prospers. Clumsy mistakes were made but I changed in the learning. When things were painful and hard, I never let myself play the victim or the martyr. To protect my energy, I am stern on being paid for my time, saying no to things that will cause me unhealthy forms of stress, and cutting loose anything that does not serve me or my higher purpose- very quickly.

"Healthy boundaries are self-care."
"You have to fill your bucket to water the seeds you wish to grow."
~Lucy Ann Delaat

I teach people how to make decisions based on what is best for their highest and best selves. In terms of being a Warrior, I teach them to pick up their sword for their truth and purpose, and not be afraid to use it. Transparently. Authentically. Fearlessly.

Carl Jung did an interesting study with women. He asked them, "Would you rather be good or whole?" Many chose good, and put 'being good and nice' above self-care. They had a tendency to deeply bury the shadow-self. Here's the short version of what doing Shadow Work is: it's all about owning your shit, and shining a big ass light on it. Enough said. Shatter your own myth of 'niceness'. There is no bigger hurdle to levelling up than not realizing you are at the center of what is happening in your life– and owning it.

If you are game, I invite you to try this on:
I am (your name), and I am not a nice person. I am a kind and assertive person, with healthy self-respect and boundaries. I claim victory over the territory of my mind, body and spirit.
I am a Warrior Queen.

The Jungian perspective guides us on our individual quest for wholeness by revealing and unmasking the Shadow part of ourselves. If we do not, and if we resist, we can destroy relationships, crush our spirits and be prevented from realizing any of our dreams. Being 'nice' is not good for anyone; it is not the same as being kind. Specifically, to yourself first, then others. Knowing your whole self is not about becoming dark. It is about saying, "I see you, and I just took your power away by calling you out. I'm going to be over here working on the good stuff, while I keep a sharp eye on you." Keep your inner friends close, but your inner enemy closer. There is Native American wisdom about feeding the White Wolf. But if you turn your back on the Shadow Wolf, it can make you miserable, silence you, and create passive aggression and much worse. It can consume you.

"Shadow Work is all about facing the jewel of the soul in all its many facets, both light and dark– and being present and aware in all aspects of the process. The transformation comes from release of ego, choosing to recognize your

wholeness, and trusting that you are part of something much bigger than yourself."
~Lucy Ann Delaat

Out of sheer loyalty, and trying to be 'nice', I had once stayed on far too long in an untenable business situation. One of my partners (and dear friend) had made several poor renegade decisions. At the top of the list was his refusal of my pleas to put contractual agreements in place on many occasions. Additionally, people were aboard our life raft that were loyal only to the need for us (the boat and oars), but not loyal to us ourselves (the rowers). I could not get the discipline or collaboration I needed for my work to have legs. I was on a floating madhouse, and became very ill. Friendships aside, I knew in my heart I needed to go self-cultivate. My home life had fallen into chaos, and my time and energies at work were functionally disrespected countless times. All this because of familiarity.

Familiarity is no excuse for unhealthy boundaries— in business or otherwise, intentionally or not. I am quick to call out what crosses a healthy boundary now, for me, or others.

There was no bad intent in the example above, but in other situations, things are indeed premeditated and involve narcissistic, sociopathic and/or dangerous personalities. Like many self-thinking types, I have also experienced being the target of sociopaths in personal and business circles. They are, of course, very skilled at engineering conflict and propaganda to isolate others who represent a threat to their ability to fully control a more naive group of people. At one point, as a young mother, I remember feeling utterly alone in world full of such people. I remember going through a particularly hard day, feeling dangerously depressed, reaching for the phone and feeling I had no friend to call I could trust. This forced me to work hard to surround myself with those who were more self-aware, less self-serving, and more loyal. I needed to be around people of my nature who stood up, not only for themselves, but when unacceptable boundaries towards others were crossed. I did, quickly, and those are the people that are in my inner circle– and are still allowed to play in my backyard treehouse. I am so successful in my close friendships; they are sacred relationships to me.

One of the many narcissists I have had to recover from in my life was a "friend" of my husbands for over 15 years. His disturbing, suggestive behavior had escalated, and he had become increasingly angry as I put up boundaries. Making the women in our group uncomfortable by sexualizing everything was one of the many ways he gained narcissistic fuel, becoming angry if he was ignored. On the last day I saw him, he was drunk and hit my arm hard after I had refused his pass at me. My husband had overheard, and later confronted him in such a way that he provided a shuddering confession– that he had premeditated it for a very long time. Everything started to make chilling sense. There were major repercussions in his life. I learned later this was patterned sexually predatory behavior for him; others in our circle had red flags go up regarding him also. "I was drunk," or, "It was just a joke," is often a precursor to assault. If something doesn't feel right, it usually isn't. Do not let familiarity allow you to let your guard down, as abusers will use this as part of their conditioning towards an assault. Men, please listen to the women in your lives when they express concern, and take action. Lives have been saved this way.

Sam

I want to talk about a boy named Sam. His family deserves privacy and peace, so I have not used his real name.

It was about six years after that day escaping my car accident, with nothing to show except a 1 cm scar at the base of my thumb, and an open mind to things unseen. I will never truly know if it is related, but in the early winter of 2004 I started dreaming of being awakened by someone shaking me, and directed to look at the field outside my window. I dismissed it as stress impacting my dreams.

Months passed. On the following Mother's Day in 2005 I was strangely insistent on taking mom for a golf cart ride to a part of the property I never went to. Later, she would tell me, I told her to stay back as I walked several meters straight into the woods, which I never do. I remember having this macabre thought that I would find a body and thinking I had watched too many crime shows. Then I saw him. It was Sam. Flashes of images I could not explain came into my head– of a party with drugs, of young men standing together– just like I was there with them. I think Sam had been prompting me to find him. The police officer said, "It's a good thing you came out here, another month and the grass would have grown so high his family would have never found him." I wept fiercely and experienced utter exhaustion that night. The dreams never returned.

Sam's mother would finally have closure after months. I have only told this whole story to a handful of close friends. Although I write fiction I couldn't make this stuff up in my own life. My mom had later confirmed she had a strange feeling looking out my bedroom window throughout that winter and spring, as well. I share this for Sam, and because it further shifted my desire to help others in times of adversity. I am humbled that I could be the channel for this peace and closure. Many hours of contemplation have been devoted to this experience, and I am sure many more will. Not a day goes by I do not think of Sam. I am so glad to devote this part of my chapter to him.

Point No Return

I share only glimpses of my journey. There have been many obstacles. And there is much more grief. The few stories I share are to convey the understanding I have come to know in my own life, and to, hopefully, enlighten yours.

At 48, in May of 2016 I was diagnosed with late Stage 3 bowel cancer. I was 'healthy'. I ate well, I exercised regularly. Friends and family were shocked. Two nightmarish weeks were spent without sleep, being led to believe death would find me before Christmas. I had been misdiagnosed for years, and they had said the weight gain and bloating that made me look like a parade balloon was premenopausal. CRC is a sneaky bastard, and hides itself well. A horror show of radiation, chemo, and two operations followed over the next 15 months. I nearly died several times, often due to medical errors, including a blood clot from a PICC line. I had an amazing surgeon, and if not for him I surely would not have survived. Hospital conditions were horrendous, I was left in a filthy room with someone else's blood on the bathroom floor, with no painkillers or water on several occasions.

After 20 hours in a hospital emergency with one near death crisis, I was left in a hallway with my temporary ostomy, which has now since been reversed. I had no washroom, save for the public one, for almost 24 hours. I 'slept' under a UV light and begged for death to take me. Instead, someone came and 'sat' with me many, many times. At times I heard angelic singing, felt invisible hands comforting me or holding me as I wept. This presence carried me through times of anguish. Despite my tenacity and threshold for pain, the psychological trauma would take its toll. I suffered PTSD for many months after, and still have the odd nightmare. Can you believe one of the hardest things was losing my hair? I did not understand why, at first, but later realized, the connection to my hair had brought back the childhood trauma I endured living with my grandparents. It felt like just one more punishment, but this, too, has healed.

My mother, father, husband and son were pillars of support. My only sister and I grew even closer than we already were. My close friends Isabel, Sandy, Lily, Sofia and the rest, as well as my healing circle, M3, and extended family, enveloped me with every form of healing. I cried as I opened the little notes in my healing basket that said wonderful things about why I was loved. They all helped save my life. A Shaolin Monk shot what felt like lightning bolts through my body with his bare hands. I practiced meditation, purging, forgiving, energy clearing, and threw unconditional love at my mind, body and spirit. I let go. I let God. I healed. I embraced my call to service and gratitude. I am fearless now, whatever comes.

And so began the long road home, the Warrior Queen resurrected, returned with the Elixir— my shareable lessons for the world.

Passing The Sword

Long before you were born, you created a purpose for yourself. Maybe the adversity in your life has caused you to take pause. There is a saying, "The difference between a weed and a flower is judgment." Everyone has their own crown of dandelions. Do you have weeds or flowers? It is up to you to decide.

We write our own chapters in our Hero's Journey. Every moment and every manifestation of our free will affects the expansion of the universe, and the collective conscious. As Rumi once said, "You are not a drop in the ocean, but the entire ocean in a single drop." You are an enormous force in the universe— whether you realize it or not. If you can come to reflect upon and understand that, you will see the world and everyone in it quite differently. I became open to recognizing forces around me at that mangled wreck all those years ago, but it has taken this most recent rollover in my life to collectively heal.

You must follow your bliss on your journey. No matter my work, I have loved the journey, as opposed to all the shiny trappings that come and go. I have become masterful in my ability to leverage adversity, and transmute it into the joy of shareable lessons in my life's work. In my work, I have come to call this "Applied Antics™." If you are shifting or purging at this point in your life, I know it is uncomfortable. But this is what finding a life on purpose is truly about! Happiness is a choice. I hope my chapter has brought you happiness and a new sense of your own power.

I will leave you with a simple mantra:

Today I choose to be happy and feel joy. I am healthy. I am enough. I am powerful. I am whole. I am grateful. I am unconditional love. Everything is always working out for me. I am open to the call.

And if you are brave enough to take the sword and join me, fierce Warrior, "How may I serve?"

Lucy Ann Balzano-DeLaat is the Co-Founder of OnBrandAgency.com. She is a Corporate Storyteller, Content Creator, and writer of award-nominated films. Lucy enjoys helping organizations leverage their challenges through her Coaching and Speaking practice, From Adversity To Success®.

A true champion will fight through anything.
~Floyd Mayweather Jr.

Jennifer Buttineau

Healing Journeys

I finally sit to write my story... I can't tell you how many times I sat and prepared to write, but couldn't. Yesterday was Summer Rosemary's second birthday. I told myself that yesterday was 'the day' as a birthday gift to her... it still took me until today.

You see, telling this story is no easy feat. My name is Jennifer and I am a Mother to two beautiful angel babies: Olivia May, who would be 5-years-old now; and, Summer Rosemary who's second birthday was yesterday. Just writing these words on paper makes my heart break... because it makes the memory so much more vivid and real to see it in black and white - even though I feel the heartache there every day.

I guess I should start off where my story of happiness and brokenness began. It was May 2012; I was 33-years-old and had never been pregnant before. I had always been told due to complications with my reproductive system that I would probably never conceive. Then miraculously I became pregnant for the very first time! I was so happy!! I was beside myself with happiness, and knew that I would do anything I had to to make sure that I was a good Mother to my precious Miracle Baby! I, myself, am an only child, and I had always wanted siblings and to have a family of my own. I adore children and am Auntie Jen to quite a few. I had been with the baby's father for a year at this point and was excited to tell him the news but, my goodness, ohhhh so scared and nervous too!! I was so nervous that I re-did a pregnancy test at my cousin Sabrina's house just to make sure before I told him.

So that night, as we lay in bed, I whispered in his ear, "I'm pregnant." Let's just say the outcome was not how I had hoped. His exact words were, "Are you kidding me?" My heart sank. Things changed... he didn't want the baby, so I became less of a priority to him. He would drink and continue on with his life, while ignoring me and barely texting. He would check in sometimes, but not much. There were times I thought he was coming around to the thought. I would invite him to ultra-sounds or appointments, but nothing. I knew I was in this alone and thought to myself, "I can do this. I don't need him; it will be me and my baby!!"

At the time I was working as a Restaurant Manager at a Marina and was working quite a few hours as my job was salary based. It was July, and at this point I had still not told my parents, the standard rule is to wait until the 12 week safety mark. I knew I didn't want to tell them and then disappoint them with a miscarriage. I knew how badly they wanted to be grandparents. They were going on vacation. I was making pretty good money and knew that I would need a nursery at their home so I thought I will do the spare room into a nursery while they are away! I wanted to surprise them when they got home... and so I did!! There was old paneling in there and shag carpet from the 70's, so I hired a good friend of mine to come in to hang drywall and tear out the rug and put in nice wood laminate flooring. I shopped with my cousin for the crib, the bedding, and all of the accessories to decorate a zoo/wild animal theme! We picked a paint color that was gender neutral (a soft buttery yellow) with cream trim. It was going to be beautiful! The nursery was almost finished, but my parents came home a couple of days early. That didn't matter because when they found out about the pregnancy, they were very excited. I think my Dad was happy to see the drywall and carpet gone! My Dad ended up finishing the trim and put the crib together. All the same it looked fantastic; a jungle themed room with palm trees, coconuts, monkeys, lions, tigers, giraffes, zebras, and more!! There was my Grandma Anderson's Rocking Chair, that holds such sentimental history, and change table by the window and it was just perfect, right down to the tiger night light plugged in the wall.

I kept working as I was saving money for the baby, but fairly soon I began to get tired and have pains in my tummy. Everyone said it was normal from my stomach stretching and the baby growing, and that tiredness was normal, too. The pains eventually got worse, and I would have to go lay down. Being a nervous Nelly and a first time mother, I went to the doctor. He advised I should go on light duty at work. Then one day at work I had really, really bad pains and had to sit down. I thought to myself that this wasn't right; pregnancy is not supposed to hurt like this. So I left work. I napped for several hours and woke up feeling fine, and thought maybe it was just a growing pain. But that day in August is a day I will never forget.

That night I went over to a friend's house to watch a movie and lie on the couch and relax, but I kept having pains in my lower back. I thought it was odd because I hadn't felt that before, and I had the urge to pee badly. With a pregnancy bladder the size of a grape, I thought I better go before the movie starts. Well, I went to the washroom and all of a sudden my water broke!!! I didn't even know what to do! I was sitting on the toilet and all I kept thinking was, "Oh my God, this is too early!! I'm only 14 weeks." So I screamed. I didn't know what else to do. It was one of the scariest moments of my life. We were 40 minutes away from the closest hospital and all I kept thinking was I'm losing the baby, I'm having a miscarriage, and I just can't lose the baby... no, no, no!!! This isn't happening... this can't be happening. No, not my baby. The drive was something that was out of a movie... we were driving sooo fast, but I felt every second of time tick by. Tick-tock. I was losing my baby and there was nothing I could do about it. Why, why was this happening to me?

We arrived at the hospital and they took me in immediately. During this time I was texting with the baby's Dad and he just kept replying that I should let him know what was happening. So I texted as I could, but he was nowhere to be seen... the feeling of being alone and scared was just overwhelming. I prayed. I prayed and I prayed. The doctor said he thought I was having a miscarriage and that I had lost almost all of my amniotic fluid when my water broke. The prognosis was not good. They brought the ultra sound machine in and, low and behold, my precious little baby had a heart beat! The doctor couldn't believe it. I cried and cried out of pure joy. I didn't lose the baby. My baby is still alive!!

But now the rest of my pregnancy complications began.

I was put on very strict bed rest. I was only able to stand up to go to the washroom or to shower (which had to be done sitting on a chair) I wasn't allowed to walk, or barely move. If I left the house it was only to go to doctor's appointments, or to the hospital. I still had not seen my baby's father this whole time. He never came to the hospital. He never came to my parent's house to visit me. He never even talked to my family about my health. He just did not care at all. I was alone and I knew it. I was bedridden and had my Mother taking care of me, cooking for me, changing me, and sometimes bathing me because I was unable to move really. I only left the house once every 5 or 6 days. Every move I made could mean amniotic fluid loss because there was a hole in the sac that carried my baby and any fluid that built in there was precious and critical to my baby's life. I went through all of that alone, watching TV, movies, and trying to stay sane by reading pregnancy books and novels and such. I had very few visitors and felt so, so very alone. I was heartbroken on top of it all, knowing that we didn't mean anything to someone that I had put so much time into. But every day I grew stronger emotionally, for me and my baby.

So as time passed, by the end of August I started feeling my baby kick. I just loved it!! I loved the feeling of being a Mom and cherished every moment as I knew it was such a special gift. I was having a miracle baby!! The doctors were still in amazed that my miracle baby was holding strong and growing.

I had regular doctor's appointments and at September 5th I had made it to 20 weeks. I finally got to have the ultra sound to find out if my little one was a boy or a girl. I guessed it would be a boy... I had wanted a boy so bad. I was so excited to see my baby on screen; my little baby with a heartbeat, and hands and toes, and such tiny little feet! My little bun in the oven didn't want to co-operate and kept her legs closed (not that I knew she was a she at this point of course). So my little baby was going to be a surprise! She even waved to us on screen! My Mom had come with me so I wasn't alone. One of the only memories she'll have as a grandmother I suppose, but none of that mattered... I was ecstatic and bought the video to take home so I could keep for baby's memories. I remember going home that night and watching it over and over. It was surreal to me to see my little love on screen. I kept looking to see if I could tell the gender, but decided a surprise baby it would be. I remember messaging her Dad and not getting much of a response. One of the happiest days of my life and no love of my life to share it with; this saddened me so. I remember feeling so alone but yet not, because I knew I had my baby and we would take on the world together!

Who knew what turn of events were about to happen....

Just days after my 20 week ultra-sound the bigger complications began. I was in such excruciating pain. I was in and out of the hospital, staying for a couple days, and then sent home. This went on for a couple weeks and they kept doing tests, but the baby was still showing no signs of distress; no complications and her heartbeat was strong! I believed. I hoped and I prayed. They had told me to be prepared for a preemie because of all of my complications and they made arrangements for my bed and my arrival at Mount Sinai Hospital for 23 weeks. My goal was to reach 26 weeks as a minimum.

So I counted down. I was bedridden and scared. I read about preemies and their stories and what could happen. I counted days, hours, weeks, and every minute was a miracle. I believed! 21 weeks... 21 weeks 2 days... 21 weeks 3 days.... I counted to 22 weeks.

September 19th I went into the hospital in premature labor They told me to hang on and to hope that it was false labor; to relax. They gave me something in an IV drip to stop my labor from progressing. They had me on morphine for the pain and drugged to keep me sedated and calm. I was unable to move. They wanted me that way. This went on for 3 more days. Drugged, laying in the hospital, no real visitors, except for my Mom and Dad occasionally and no sight of my baby's father. I had texted him and told him exactly what was going on. He lived only 10 minutes away, but our baby and I were not reason enough to drive over to see how we were doing.

I remember thinking, "Baby it's you and me, and I love you and we need 2 more days before we have a bed in Mount Sinai. We have to hold on. We have to stay strong. I love you my baby and we're going to make it through this. Mommy loves you sooo very, very much. You are my world. We are going to have an amazing life together!!"

I was in labor for 51 hours. I delivered naturally a beautiful little girl who I named Olivia May. I still remember the doctor saying it's a girl... I was actually shocked because I had wanted a boy. But none of that mattered as she was so beautiful and precious in my eyes. I named her Olivia after my Dad (the girls version of his name) and May after one of my best girlfriends.

I'll never forget the last moments of being pregnant. I had said to the nurse I feel pressure down there and she checked and said, "The baby's head is crowning. I'm so sorry." She called the doctor and they kept telling me everything that was going to happen. They tried to prepare me for the outcome because my baby was coming too soon. I kept saying no. I was alone. I had no one I knew there with me. Just doctors and nurses. They wheeled me to the delivery room and they kept preparing me for what the outcome was going to be. I had a nurse, whose name I don't even know, hold my hand through it all; during my contractions, my pushes, and my delivery. She held my hand and squeezed it tight and I remember her telling me, "I'm here, I'm here." I delivered Olivia May on Saturday, September 22, 2012 at 12:06pm. She weighed 14 ounces, just shy of 1 pound. I watched her breathe her last breath and knew I would never be the same again.

The nurse brought me Olivia May wrapped in a small purple and white crocheted blanket with a little pink crocheted hat. I held her in my arms as long as they would let me. One of the nurses (again whose name I have no memory of - just another nurse angel sent to me) came and took pictures of me and my baby girl. These are the only ones I will ever have of her. They made me baby keepsakes with handprints and footprints, and it is just so special and dear to my heart.

They kept me in the hospital for 2 days after, drugged and sedated. I was isolated in the maternity ward in my own room, so I didn't have to see the other mothers with their newborn babies. But they couldn't shut out the sounds. I could still hear the babies' cries. There was another mother in there at the same time that lost her baby as well. I heard the talk in the halls. We had different stories, but the same outcome. Her baby was carried full term, a 10lb baby boy... he had the umbilical cord wrapped around his neck during delivery and it strangled him. The brutal reality was that both of us as mothers had to face that we carried our babies, loved our babies, ate healthy for our babies and loved them so. We both went home from the hospital without them, with empty arms and broken hearts, and dreams of what could have been.

During my stay in the hospital I saw no one but my Mom and Dad and two girlfriends, Sheila and Michelle, who were both nurses at the hospital. I didn't want to see anyone. I had no happy ending to share. Just a sad, broken-hearted one. I was alone.

After losing Olivia I went numb. I was lost. I went through the motions and tried to pretend I was fine. I had a small funeral for Olivia at the funeral home. The only ones that were there to say goodbye were me and my mother. Her own father didn't show any interest in even coming. I found out later that he never even told his parents that I was pregnant... and yet I still forgave him. I had loved him at one point and still did somehow.

He invited me over after losing the baby, but there was no mention of what I had gone through. He was in denial. We hung out for a few weeks, but I really only went over because I was so sad and didn't want to be alone. I remember saying these exact words to him, "I'm worried I'm going to go on a downward spiral." He didn't say much. It was one of the last times I saw him during that time. He couldn't handle how broken I was. So instead of helping me... out of sight, out of mind right?

So, I did what I had to do; I got strong. I got focused and just said fuck it!! I'm leaving and I'm going on a healing journey. I'm going backpacking in Central America! I texted him to let him know and he said, "Do what you need to do." He let me leave without even one question asked. I bought my plane ticket, with knowing only one friend down in Nicaragua through Facebook, and off I went! I didn't know a single word of Spanish and had no idea really where Nicaragua even was... all I knew is that I liked his pictures and it looked beautiful. I was going to learn to surf! November 18th I landed in Managua, one of the busiest cities there, and didn't speak any Spanish so that was fun telling the taxi where I needed to go. I stayed in a dodgy hotel room with prostitutes and drug dealers out front waiting for the bus in the morning. I didn't care though. Not one little bit! Because I wasn't anywhere near home where the pain was. The girl at the front desk told me when the Discotheque started at night to stay in my room and lock the doors. Of course I had to see... so I went. I saw guns, drug dealers, pimps and more; but it did not scare me, because they could not touch the pain that I felt. They had nothing on my broken heart.

The next morning I took the bus to San Juan del Sur. I found paradise!! I met up with the only person I knew in the country, and met him face to face for the first time ever. But everything was fine. We stayed in a lovely hostel right across from the beach. My days became sunny again, I started to walk the beach, I journaled daily, met new people, experienced life... after all I hadn't been out of the house for months other than to doctors and hospitals. So this was a new found FREEDOM to me!!

I had planned on being in Central America for a couple of weeks and experiencing a few different countries... that sure did change real fast. I extended my flight for just over a month. I was FREE. FREE from feeling hurt and pain. FREE from peoples stares, condolences and asking where the baby was, did I have a boy or girl, or people not knowing what to say so they just wouldn't talk to me at all. I was getting another chance at LIFE. A chance to heal.

From there I went to the Isla of Ometepe that is an island created by two volcanoes in the only fresh water lake in Nicaragua. There were jungles, volcanoes to hike, waterfalls to play in, rivers to kayak, springs to swim in, untouched purity of life with dirt roads with palm trees and monkeys! This Island is like no other, like a time warp going back 100 to 200 years... I remember thinking to myself as I walked alone on one particular beach Olivia brought me here. I found untouched paradise and saw almost identical palm trees with coconuts just like the ones on her nursery wall. I saw monkeys, also just like the ones on her nursery wall. I knew that she was with me on this journey. I knew she was healing me from within. She was telling me it was okay and that I wasn't alone. I could feel it.

After Nicaragua I bounced from country to country, taking buses and staying in hostels throughout Central America. It was amazing. I went to Costa Rica on the Caribbean side to a town called Puerto Viejo where I met two of the coolest people from England and Scotland that I am still friends with to this day! We then continued to travel together; busing to Panama and going to Bocas Del Toro and Red Frog Beach. I was a border hopper and backpacker now, traveling with nothing but my 'Rojo Grande' (Big Red, in Spanish) suitcase. We played in the waves and on the beaches! We were FREE and that is all that mattered.

From Panama I went back up to Costa Rica, stayed a while in a little town called Dominical and learned to surf. I had no idea this town would become such a HUGE part of my life but, here, I made new friends from Texas who would become my adopted American family up until this very day! From there I bused back to Nicaragua, went to Granada, then to a desolate Island and Turtle Sanctuary where I helped release hundreds – and possibly thousands – of baby sea turtles into the ocean!! I rode horseback in the moonlight on the beach, sang by the fire with surfers and new friends. Then it was off to Leon where I climbed and boarded down the side of Cerro Negro, the second most active volcano in Central America. It's rated as #2 on CNN's thrill seekers bucket list, and #4 on the top 10 death defying destinations. Speeds up to 90km/hr. racing down the side of an active volcano!! The thing is none of that mattered to me. I had no fear. I was numb. I was untouchable because to me nothing could hurt me more than the loss of my baby girl. I was a mother with no child. So even being covered in lava dust I was smiling ear to ear! You only get to live ONCE and in my eyes from the day I lost Olivia May I was going to grab life by the MF'ing balls and live LIFE for her!! Everything I did, every step I took was now to experience everything that she could not. Every scent, every touch, every feel and experience... EVERYTHING. I had a new inner strength in me and I was untouchable. I felt invincible.

I decided to fly home for Christmas as I knew my parents were worried about my well-being in Central America, especially knowing that I was grieving the loss of my daughter. So I was going home for Christmas for them.

December 20th I boarded my flight to go home for the holidays. I went straight to an all-girls Christmas party to deliver presents that I had bought on my travels for some of my very best of girlfriends. We had drinks, chatted and danced, and I told stories of my adventures. My girlfriends knew I was stronger. They could see it. They knew that I had found this place inside that was untouchable.

After leaving the party I got home with Rojo Grande tired from the travel; within minutes of arriving home I found out the devastating news of my ex-boyfriend and my soulmate Andrew passing away while I was on flight in the air. My heart stopped beating for a moment. I now knew that my healing journey to overcome the death of my daughter was for something even more. My heart now knew a different pain and a different death.... I screamed. I didn't want to believe it but I knew what I had to do. I became a fucking warrior! I put my armor on and I did what I had to do. I put together picture collages and told memories at the funeral on Christmas Day. We buried him two days later on my birthday, December 27th.

These past 5 years have been one hell of a ride. I went back to Olivia's Father and forgave him. I have lost yet another daughter with him since. I called her my little Peanut. On December 14, 2015 at 9:51am I gave birth naturally to another beautiful baby girl I named Summer Rosemary. Summer because she brought me sunshine like my favorite season and Rose after my Memere (Roseanne was her middle name, Ann is mine) and Mary after my Mother's middle name and their other Grandmothers.

Heaven gained another one of my Angels. She weighed only 390 grams. I carried her 22 ½ weeks - a most exactly the same amount of days as Olivia. I was in labor with her for about 27-30 hours, with the same sad outcome and, yes, the same sad story involving him. Life repeated itself. I was very alone once again, and have not seen him since the day after Summer Rosemary was born.

I lost both of my babies due to not being able to carry them properly, due to part of my cervix being removed prior due to cervical cancer. I am a cancer survivor. In saving me, I lost them... and that is something I have to live with daily.

Since losing Summer I have become what I consider to be an Ultimate Warrior and I found strength within me I never knew I even had. I have sailed across oceans and traveled to amazing new places. I am stronger than I have ever been. They are my Strength.

Through every new adventure and journey, through every trip I take, I do it for them. I carry three hearts within me.

Jennifer Buttineau- a Free Spirited Gypsy Soul who loves children, animals, boating and playing in the water, nature and being active outdoors. Her true passion is travel and she is an adventurer at heart!

Through heartbreaks and pains, she firmly believes in never taking life for granted. Life is a very precious gift... Embrace every moment.

She is a Mother. She is a SURVIVOR. She is a WARRIOR!!

"You can't change your past, but you can make your future amazing!" "YOLO!!"

Jacqui Childs

Lost and Found

The Devil whispers, "You cannot withstand the storm."
The Warrior replies, "I am the Storm."
~Unknown

Not The Fairy Tale

I watched as he packed up my past; everything and anything seemed to fit nicely in a large green garbage bag. I assume he thought if my photos, portfolio, magazines, etc. were all gone I would be a brand new person. There was to be no past or anything unsavory for friends or family to find (this was way before social media), so a garbage bag was a lot like a delete button; the final destination of my dirty past was the city dump or 'empty recycle bin'.

To be completely fair I was very excited! I actually thought this was a fabulous idea. I couldn't believe someone so awesome wanted to be with me, even knowing that I wasn't exactly Mother Teresa! Heck, I wasn't sure I'd be able to be a mother at all after years of use and abuse.

So here is where I share what was in the garbage bag. Trying to hide who I was wasn't one of the greatest moments of my life (still 20 years later I'm not known for making great decisions). It was only magazines, trading cards, calendars, tiny bikinis, and fancy clothes. All tricks of the trade, but as I matured and grew I realized what was really packed up that day were my hopes and dreams; pride and dignity, love and faith in mankind. Without those 'things' I felt truly alone in this world.

Now I don't want to give "him" or any of them too much time, as this story is mine after all. Most of the 'hims' in my life had always taken their fair share, and taken what was rightfully mine as well. As long as I could remember I never felt as If I belonged, I was always on the outside looking in, or so distant I couldn't be heard. You know when you try to listen with water in your ears and you hear a strange echo? Or that tunnel you shout into that makes you sound far away? That is how I can best describe my voice— distant. Like no one can hear me, or better yet, they hear me but they don't listen, and they didn't care.

"You see I usually find myself among strangers because I drift here and there trying to forget the sad things that happened to me."
~ F. Scott Fitzgerald

New World

I was finally old enough to start my new life. At 19, I packed up and moved to a new city. I would go to school, get a job, make new friends and create a 'new world'. This time I would be in charge, or so I thought. I wouldn't fall into old routines and the wrong crowd wasn't an option; rebirth.

My 'new world' city was a lot warmer and seemed to have so much more to offer. I would grab a bus to school, wait in a really long line to register, stop at the book store to grab some books, hop back on the bus and start looking for a job. That would be normal, and I would definitely feel like I belonged.

Once again on that first day of school I felt like an outsider. How could that be? No one knew me here; I was just like every other kid standing around looking lost. What I did notice though were all the minivans and station wagons out front. I could hear the last minute words of encouragement; I saw the smiles, waves and tears. Once again there wasn't anyone there for me.

That first day I decided to walk home; it was still warm and light out, however it was longer than I had thought. It started to get a little dark and being new to the area I was kind of nervous to keep walking. I decided to hop on the next bus and stayed on for a few stops. I got off when I thought I was close enough. My bags were heavy, my feet were sore and, as usual, my mind was wandering. No doubt I was making plans for my new life; I had so much to do, starting with the basics like feeding myself.

While in 'Never Never Land' as I walked towards what was known to some as "Crack Alley" I suddenly fell to the ground! What did I trip on? Did someone just push me? Yep!

Welcome to your 'new world'.

When he finished and left me, I jumped up and looked all around – not to find help, but to see if anyone was watching. I was so embarrassed. How could this be happening here? I had always thought it was "them"; was it me?

I showered and wiped myself off with a Clorox wipe as I had done many times in the past. I thought about calling the police, or going to the hospital, but I had so much to do and those places were for victims – the weak or sick – and I was never going to be one of them.

I was about a week into school and money from babysitting and loans had been running low. I thought to myself this weekend I definitely needed to look for a job. I walked downtown and went into a tanning salon. I wanted to apply for a job, but as usual my anxiety picked then to rear its ugly head. I went for a tan instead, and when I went up to the counter to pay I heard, "Did you want the dancer rate?" Did she just assume I was a stripper?

I spent the next two weeks applying for jobs and going to school very late, or not at all, drinking anything I could find and walking to soup kitchens or food banks to get some bread and peanut butter. My mother's great advice was I could get anything I wanted with my good looks.

Secrets of the Past

My mom was a nice enough lady (most of the time). However, she was so wrapped up in her own world. And my sister, if you can believe it, well... I was the good kid! Totally normal.

Our relationship has been interesting through lots of laughs and tears; somehow along the way she became an enemy - or maybe she always was? I don't know. Mothers and daughters seem to have a strange dynamic. I know what I had hoped for might have been a fairytale but I had always thought a mother was your biggest fan, your defender above all others, or at least would just be there for me.

I guess those Harlequin romances were way more interesting than I was. Oh well, we did have a lot of laughs. Maybe she's just a victim of her generation, but drowning in her 'poor me' negativity wasn't the healthiest place for me. Let's add that my mother's version of the story would be quite different than mine. I guess that's why they say there are two sides to every story.

Since I gave my mom a minute in this story I guess I should mention my dad. He fed us, clothed us, and scared the crap out of us every chance he got. I should forgive and forget, but he did throw me out of a moving car onto the highway, and that's not even the half of it. I think it's been over 20 years since we last spoke; probably my fault (in his eyes I'm sure). Lucky for him I keep his secrets in a vault where there aren't any windows or doors.

"You will always be fond of me. I represent to you all the sins you never had the courage to commit."
~Oscar Wilde

Enter Shawn

"Ladies and gentleman I'd like to introduce to you, Shawn Knight!" Wow! Putting that name on paper just gave me that shock and awe feeling like a dead relative reappeared.

After weeks of looking for a job, dropping out of school, and eating in soup kitchens I decided to take a little bit of my mother's advice, but I'm pretty sure this wasn't what she intended with her pep talk. Ta da!! Shawn was born in this 'new world'. And, yes, she was taking and having anything and anyone she wanted, just like mamma said I could.

Shawn was fascinating; she was my alter ego, my superhero. Once she came along I had food on the table, shoes on my feet, and men pounding down my door. I guess Jacqui checked out while Shawn ran amuck all over town, and by town I guess I meant my 'new world'. Anywhere Shawn went, all was right.

Even my grandparents reaped the benefits. I became Santa Claus at all the holidays, showering everyone with gifts and no one asked questions. I was modeling bikinis and lingerie, or so I told my family. From time to time Shawn would take a 'me day' and try to figure out where and how this would all end. I knew this kind of life never ended well. At least none of the girls I knew were on to bigger and better things, unless bigger and better was porn or death.

Back to Innocence

It was the late 90's. I missed my hometown; friends were beginning to get married, graduate and start 'real life'. I thought it might be time to return home now that I was a stronger, wiser person; I definitely couldn't be messed with.

I would keep Shawn in my back pocket and try not to ever pull her out.

Back in my small town there was no way I would survive. I was bored to tears so I called upon my 'old friends' and went right back to where I left off. Oh, my 'old friends' - they were Coke, Acid, Mushrooms, and Alcohol, and we partied often. It didn't really matter if no one else was around.

Back at home there was one strip club and since I was already the talk of town, there was no reason not to just jump right in. I bought a car, and a house, and left a string of men with their heads spinning. It was way easier to live here as Shawn. She was of the mindset 'do it to them before they do it to you', which was working really well. Even in this world, I didn't exactly fit in; I dated the owners, the banker, the butcher, the baker, the candlestick maker; you get the point.

The girls at work would come to me for advice, or try to befriend me, but I wasn't one of them. I was better - or at least I thought I (Shawn) was.

I was getting tired of the long days and the late nights and I so desperately wanted to be normal (whatever that was). I tried again and again with my family, but one wrong answer, or a roll of the eyes from any of them, and I'd disconnect them from my world again. Who are we kidding though? They really didn't know much about me or my world; did they even care to?

Another Try at Me

I was back to my 'new life' activities again; walking blocks and blocks looking for a job, going into every bar or restaurant I could find. Finally, a man heard me on the phone with a friend asking where I should apply next. He tapped me on the shoulder and said, "My friend is looking for a bartender." YES! I can eat tonight. For a few short weeks I slept at a girlfriend's house and worked at the bar in the day. It was easy, maybe too easy; I found it a little boring.

I dated a lot of different men from all over. Remember this was before social media, so learning to be social and act human was very important in my line of work (what's a nice way to label that 'career'?)

By this time dancer Shawn was a distant memory, and plain bartender Jacqui, with a heart of stone, was doing her best to survive. I still was searching for normal. I just wanted a family, to live a fairytale with a happy ending. Don't we all?

Secrets After the Garbage Bag

By this stage of life, I knew what I wanted and what I didn't want. I also knew what I was good at and what I wasn't. It turns out, I'm a natural chameleon, and I'm also a fabulous secret keeper. I'm not sure if the many men in my life had taught me to keep secrets – or was it my mother? One thing I know for absolute certain is if it wasn't for "him" I would never have had to use both of my gifts so frequently.

Soon after settling into 'normal' life, I became pregnant and that was an absolute blessing in disguise! Unfortunately, soon after our wedding he also shared that he wasn't exactly who he portrayed himself to be. Had I known better, I would have run for the hills.

But, as usual, no one was there for me, and there was no 'hill' in sight. That was an entirely new nightmare that I will keep stored away for now.

My son was born and we played house as best we could. He kept us busy, and before long his brother was born. I fooled myself into thinking life was normal, and I finally had my family and a fairytale. Time went on, and we grew more and more apart. I was changing. People would come into my life and compliment me on my kindness, thoughtfulness, or parenting (that always meant so much more than looks). I started to seek out friends from the past, anyone who wanted to talk or listen. I didn't know it at the time, but I was deeply depressed. The years of abuse and keeping secrets was eating me up inside. Each night when it was quiet my head and heart would go to war. My children were the only thing keeping me alive.

Drinking and prescription drugs became my friend again, and I kept my circle very small. "He" was in his own world, full of bullshit and lies. I just wanted out!

*'The only difference between the saint and the sinner is
that every saint has a past, and every sinner has a future."
~Oscar Wilde*

The Fairytale was Over

I began having an affair and by no means was either of us looking for love. We were filling time. Sharing a laugh and listening to each other. He heard me. After several scary months, and years of what I know now was abuse, I gathered up the courage to leave. That was a very terrifying time. I left with no clothes, no possessions, no money, nothing - not even my children. If I ever was going to take my own life now would be the time.

The afternoon I went into my lawyer's office to sign off on EVERY-THING was devastating. I looked down at a piece of paper that basically said my 'worth', or 'value', in the marriage after 14 years, 2 beautiful boys, and years of abuse was only $30,000.00. I think I only received a check for $5500 total.

From that day forward I decided there would come a time when ALL the secrets that I held because of shame or embarrassment would be set free. I am, and will be, more than anyone has ever given me credit for, my looks or sexuality will not be what I'm known for, but for the secrets that I've kept for far too long.

Now married to the gentlemen I was having the affair with, my oldest son lives with me, and the youngest became a casualty of divorce. It has been years since I have heard his voice. I do see his beautiful face in my dreams almost every night.

Looking Back to Look Forward

I look back and watch the story of my life unfold. It is almost like a movie. I know where I went wrong and what would have helped. Had I not had to go it alone, had I not held onto so many secrets like they were family, things might be have been very different.

I started this new journey (writing) as a sort of therapy, so I could share my secrets, set them free and release them from my mind and my soul. I feel as if I have lived a hundred lives. I just want to live one. This one. I believe in order to do that it's time to share. I have learned what the words 'family' and 'friend' mean. I understand now that to truly be free, part of a family, and a good friend to myself and others, I will slowly peel it all away.

I look around and know I'm seen, but more than that I must be heard. During some of the darkest, scariest times in my life, I knew I would survive; I would be okay. I knew I would be more than

"Shawn" or a pretty wife. Even though my depression took a large part of my life, I learned a lot from it, and I'm still learning.

You never know just what greatness can come out of darkness and shame. I used it for strength like a cape I wear when I need to be brave. Would I suggest an affair, become a stripper, do drugs, keep rape and abuse quiet? Never! Talk! Shout! Scream! until someone listens. Someone will hear you.

As I begin to come to the end of my chapter I feel as if I am saying goodbye to a friend, like I am moving away. It has been quite an experience to open old doors and windows. I've really only touched the surface, but now that those windows and doors are open I think I've found the courage to leave them open and see what healing comes. I know the outcome of my writings won't always be positive, but that's not what it's about. It is to help me heal and find my 'normal'.

Writing also allows me to become part of something bigger than myself, somewhere I can feel safe to share without shame or judgment; a family.

Thank you for listening. Just knowing someone has heard me and knows "I was" means more to me than you, as the reader, will ever know.

When I started to write, I changed direction a few times. If you can believe it, I thought my most powerful or authentic story would be a suicide letter. But while taking this time to write and search within myself, it is the past and "Shawn" that are laid to rest.

I want to live, now more than ever. I have so much more to share and so many more stories to tell. I can't wait to write for you again.

"All I wanted was to live a life where I could be me, and be okay with that. I had no need for material possessions, money or even close friends with me on my journey. I never understood people very well anyway, and they never seemed to understand me very well either. All I wanted was my art and the chance to be the creator of my own world, my own reality. I wanted the open road and new beginnings every day."
~Charlotte Eriksson

Jacqui Childs has been in and around the Social Media world for the last few years. Jacqui's Social Media has grown into the millions. Having been published over 40 times nationally and internationally she has become recognized not only for her provocative images, but also for her 'speak before thinking' attitude. To add thought to her images Jacqui began writing for online magazines in addition to her own scripts for her segments on Naked News.

Jacqui's online presence has continued to grow. While captivating the male audience, this wife and mother, sister and friend, knew she had a story inside her that "real" women could understand and relate to. At the age of 44 Jacqui has decided to share with the world she is much more than a pretty face.

After being abused for most of her life, the "real" world always seemed like a scary and dangerous place for her. Jacqui's secrets have been kept locked away in her mind, while keeping her 'locked' in her own home, leaving only to make appearances for work.

The Warrior Goddess path can show you how to honor your fear while simultaneously nourishing your power.
~Heatherash Amara

Lucia Colangelo

Non Ti Scordar Di Me (Forget Me Not)

The Legend
(How the Forget Me Not Flower Got Its Name - Author's Version)

The Knight gazed lovingly at his Lady, seeking her eyes but finding them cast downwards in shyness. He was infatuated; mesmerized by chocolate eyes, deep with warmth, and hair so black the night blinded beside it. She was tiny and delicate, like the flowers that grew abundantly by the river they were strolling beside. They were an unfamiliar species, one he had never seen before. He marveled at their bravery, growing so dangerously close to the river that was known for its ravaging waters. The Knight ached to see his Lady smile, to see the shyness fade away. He glanced at the tiny blue flowers swaying in the breeze, their petals like mouse ears tempting him. Laughing, he left her side in the hopes that a bouquet of the wild mysterious floret would award him with her sweet smile. Glancing back and seeing her face brighten at his antics gave him courage to venture closer to the edge of the riverbank. The flowers seemed to lure him wickedly with their dancing as he gathered them. Encouraged by the sweet sound of her laughter he turned towards her, arms outstretched with the finished bouquet. Suddenly he felt his feet shift in the wet, muddy bank and as his smile turned to surprised shock, his Lady's laughter turned to screams. Instinctively he threw the bouquet at her as he hit the raging water. As the tides hurled him further away from his love, he used his very last breath to plead with her, "Non ti scordar di mé!!" "Forget me not!!" ... and she never would.

In the way of all love stories... there is never an end. Love will forever be felt, not only in the hearts of the lovers, but by anyone who was lucky enough to feel the warmth of its flame.

Pine Hills Cemetery (The Present 2018)

The sun was falling, casting a golden glow on the stones proclaiming tributes to loved ones. Raffaele knelt, digging gently in the dirt. They didn't live very long in the tiny garden, but that didn't matter to him. He would just plant them again; the blue of the flower, stark against his dirty hands, matching perfectly with the color of his eyes. He glanced at the picture that didn't do justice to her spirit he could feel floating around him; his one true love, Apollonia. He had promised her he wouldn't follow her, that he would hold his broken heart together for their family. And he didn't break promises.

She had not been able to keep her vow, to grow old with him, but she had not been given a choice. She fought hard until the end; her tiny frame no indication of her strength. But it had consumed her with its savage appetite. Cancer. The killer of dreams. And the creator of Warriors.

Raffaele sighed and straightened up slowly, gazing with eyes saddened from tears of sorrow wept on her sparkly tombstone. He reached into his pocket for the familiar rustle of pink tissue, worn out and tattered from the years, and unraveled it to reveal the treasure inside; the faded blue petals of long ago, a young girl's innocent token, a legacy of love. As a monarch butterfly fluttered around, he spoke to her from his heart, "These are for you signora mia, your favorite flower, the forget me not...non ti scordar di mé," and he never would.

As Raffaele's eyes followed the monarch to the heavens, it was like the whisper of its wings had released the memories from his heart... and he remembered.

Orsara di Puglia, Italy (1957)

Raffaele had set off early that morning with his mother and three younger sisters from his home town of Monteleone di Puglia to visit with their family in Orsara. The small neighboring town was alive with the sounds of Sunday cooking. As he walked the worn-down streets Raffaele breathed deeply, the aromas floating from the open windows and doors heavy with spiciness as they chased each other around teasing and enticing. Tomato sauce, thick and heavy with the essence of basil, parsley, oregano, onion and garlic simmered on gas stoves crowded with assorted pots of meats, vegetables and risotto, all competing to be the favorite. The starchy scent of boiling pasta spiraled upwards from its salty bath with each stir of the wooden spoon. Oven doors slammed impatiently in anticipation, the pizza heavy with heaps of mozzarella di bufala. Bottles of vino ready to be savored in the celebration of family.

Raffaele saw her then, sitting on the stone steps of her home, and he was infatuated. Mesmerized by hair so black the night was bright beside it, warm brown eyes that held innocence and light. Her girlish prettiness hinting at the beauty she would become. Tiny and delicate, like the flowers she was holding; non ti scordar di mé, forget me not. And he knew he never would.

Her name was Apollonia. His youthful heart aligned in that moment with the beat that was her heart. The echo of their combined rhythm would be their link, heard across the miles, in their souls. It was true love at first sight, but destined to be separated, torn apart by continents. Yet the bouquet she held tightly against her heart sighed messages of fidelity, defying separation with the bond of true love. The legend had stamped the tiny buds with that honor and time had marked it true.

As Raffaele walked by Apollonia, he ached to see her smile, but her eyes were cast downwards in shyness. They had seen each other before, it was true, when he had visited her town on other occasions but only words in childish play had been exchanged. Today the colors in the air were pale with poignancy. Raffaele had come to say 'arrivederci', 'see you later', because in Italy, it was never goodbye. He went up the stairs to the home of his aunt, feeling Apollonia's eyes rise up from the ground to follow him until he went through the door and she couldn't anymore.

Apollonia had felt the warmth of Raffaele's captivating blue eyes, shivering at the coldness of their absence, his black hair already hinting at his rebel good looks. Even at fifteen years old, she knew... actually felt, that their certainty had been written by the stars. That their inevitable separation was just a shift in the path of their destiny... they would be together someday... she would catch hold of that feeling... and grasp it with her whole being... until they were meant to be.

Raffaele was greeted with the loudness of his relatives. The table laden with fresh fruit picked in abundance from neighboring farms, cheeses crafted by hands of the locals, pasta dressed with a tangy sauce that had simmered with the juices of ripe tomatoes and baskets of freshly baked bread. It was a luncheon filled with laughter, teasing and tears. Grand tales, told in awe of a land far away, whispered in hushed voices... sacrifice, hard work, jobs, and a better life... words of hope spoken for the land that would bring opportunity to those that sought it.

While the bitter, dark espresso with the delicate crema on top was being served to the adults in the traditional demitasse Raffaele, his sisters, and cousins, held out larger mugs to receive only a drop of the dense liquid; warm foamy milk would be added, almost overflowing with generosity. But it was the biscotti that was most anticipated; crunchy double baked cookies with slivers of almonds. Dipping them into the warm drink, the children laughed as they raced to eat the soggy treats before they plunged into the milky bath. It was a meal Raffaele would think of fondly through the years when homesick for his land, his family, and his youth.

Raffaele was getting into the car that would take him home, sad that he had not had another chance to see Apollonia, afraid that he would never see her again. When he felt her presence behind him he turned and was awarded with her shy smile. She handed him the freshly picked blue floweret, and as he held them close to his heart, as she had done, it was the words she whispered that he would never forget... that were branded in his heart forever, "non ti scordar di mé". And he never would.

Separated by Continents (The Journey to a New Land –1957)

On the deck of the SS Constitution, fifteen-year-old Raffaele held the rail tightly. He would be arriving in New York City in nine days. From there he would take the train through the long night to his new home, Toronto, Canada. His father and two older brothers would be waiting for him at the train station. They had traveled ahead months earlier to find jobs and a place to live. Now it was Raffaele's turn. Scared and excited, he was also nervous about leaving his mother and sisters alone in Italy until they could finally follow the men and be reunited in their new homeland.

As the ship left the land of his birth, Raffaele understood he was leaving behind his boyhood. Gently he took out the pink tissue in his pocket and carefully unraveled it; inside the bright blue of the flower calmed him. He knew what he had to do; he knew he would be back for her because a part of him would remain in a small town in rural Italia, in the heart of his Apollonia.

Le Lettere D'amore (The Love Letters) (1957 to 1962)

Envelopes worn and faded to yellow, tied together with tattered twine, the blue and red border instantly recognizable as air mail;

letters proclaiming love, hope and dreams. They were the start of their journey together, even though so far apart. The letters were all they had to keep their love alive, the connection their souls sought. Waiting expectantly for the mail to arrive, sometimes for weeks, then hastily but gently prying open flaps that had been sealed with wanting lips that would rather be kissing. Surprise treasures, keepsakes of memories shared... locks of hair, dried flowers, scribbled poems written on scraps... inserted with love. Romance kept alive by the power of the simple word.

For true love does exist... promises are kept... dreams do come true... young love real enough to weather time and distance. Soulmates bound by destiny, emotions intense, yet strangely calm, seek no urgency... for what was meant to be... is.

(Snippets from letters-translated from Italian) Cara Apollonia... Caro Raffaele

... your words have stayed in my heart as my memory of you has also...

... I would be honored if you accepted my promise that we will be together someday...

... it is so beautiful here! So exciting, people everywhere...

... my job at the King Edward hotel is going well...

... I bought a barber shop...

... I miss you so much...

... I enjoy reading about your life so far away...

... I am working hard here, helping my family with the land, sewing for the ladies of the town...

... when I see the flowers the same blue of your eyes my heart rejoices...

... yes my love, I will marry you...

... I am awaiting your arrival anxiously...

The Proposal (1962)

Raffaele gently laid the ring on the delicate blue petals; elegant in its simplicity he knew it would complement his new bride. Rewrapping the pink tissue carefully he placed it in his jacket pocket. He was leaving for the airport shortly to board the plane that would take him to Apollonia. In a week they would be back in Toronto, planning their wedding and starting their life together as husband and wife. Five years apart may have faded the brightness of the blue petals, but it had not paled the love that would only deepen in the coming years.

Ciao Lucia

I like to say I was born a princess... one whose tiara has fallen slightly askew through the years. But then I remember the legacy of my parents' love... a love I was created from... and I wear the crooked crown with pride. My parents are Raffaele and Apollonia, and I Lucia, am their first born daughter. My sister Giovanna was born a few years later. Life wasn't easy for the newly married young couple. My daddy was fairly settled here in Toronto by the time my mama came, but she struggled with missing her parents and family, learning a new language, finding work with no skills. My daddy had his own business, so he worked hard and long hours. They studied to get their Citizenship because they wanted to be proud Canadian parents for us. Life wasn't the fluffy pure white of fairy tales; it was messy... and colorful. I was born about two weeks after my parents' twenty-second birthdays; their love grew to embrace me too. Through the years the colors sharpened and sometimes dulled, but their love never dimmed. In fact, it grew stronger with adversity... because it was never about love... that was one thing they knew they had for sure.

Mount Sinai Hospital September 2004

The aroma of coffee reached us before the elevator stopped. I would never be able to enter a Second Cup coffee shop again after that day; the smell makes me nauseous with memories. My emotions drowning me with the sorrow I had just been forced into. I knew my sister felt the same. I saw it in the timid way she ordered her coffee, almost afraid that the evil would spread if we disturbed it with sound. So, we respected it with silence. I heard our names being called and turned to see my cousins. The turmoil in my body erupted as we hugged, sobbing tears drowning the words we didn't need to say. The killer of dreams swirled happily around us, dirtying us with its evil dust, chanting the words that pierced with its raspy voice... lung cancer, lung cancer, lung cancer.

Princess Margret Hospital December 22, 2005

Mama was restless tonight. She had suffered through another brain scan, terrified of the dark tunnel, the loudness. They brought her back to us agitated, inconsolable, we cried with her, helpless, hating the pain cancer was bullying her with. I hugged her tiny fragile body in my arms until finally screaming for the nurses to give her something to calm her down. The results had shown that the cancer which had invaded her lungs had now settled, and was contently multiplying, in her brain. The tests were being done not so that she could be helped, that hope had died when I had watched my daddy, with shaking hands and dry tears, sign the DNR, 'Do Not Resuscitate', yesterday evening. But mama's wish had been to allow the doctors to learn all they could from the body that had betrayed her.

It was strange, not hearing the whooshing hiss of the oxygen machine, the trial medication she had just completed had shrunk her tumor enough to breathe without it. But her mind was fading away. My daddy sat by mama's side, stooped low so he could feel her breath on his face. His hands gently stroking her head where the springy black curls had seared to nothing. He whispered with such tenderness that it calmed her. She stared into his blue eyes mesmerized by his words, unable to speak she reached for his face, touching, stroking. His words echoed in the silence of the room, "Sei cosi bella," "You are so beautiful," "Mia bella moglie," "My beautiful wife," "Ti amo, ti amo tanto," "I love you, I love you so much". As I watched my daddy cherish my mama, I tasted tears, salty and warm. If tears are the sounds of the soul why are they silent?

Then mama became agitated again, kicking off the covers and frantically pulling at the diaper the nurse had insisted on tonight. Suddenly, her voice gained strength for just one word, "Pee." She repeated it over and over, "Pee," "Pee," and she pointed to the washroom door. We tried to tell her it was alright, that she could go in the diaper, but she grew more and more distressed. She felt degraded, embarrassed, and ashamed; when so much has already been taken you grasp at the little you have left.

That was when my daddy, the pain so evident on his face, tore off the diaper, picked his Apollonia up in his arms and carried her for her dignity. I watched as he walked the short distance to the washroom, her body frail under the bulk of the blankets keeping her warm because her body no longer could. I remember my daddy lifting her into his arms, arms weak from exhaustion, yet strong from love. As the blanket she was wrapped in fell away, exposing her back, I remember staring at the bones jutting through skin so fine, so fragile, like lace, blue from the veins that still fed life through her. Her tailbone shocking me, just like another skeleton in this place. Where was my mama who used to complain jokingly about her chubby tummy acquired from years of indulging her sweet tooth? Where was my mama? As she was carried away by my daddy our eyes sought each other... and I saw her! She was here! My beautiful mama was inside those eyes that had mesmerized my daddy all those years ago as young love took hold. And I exhaled... and smiled at her. Her face was frozen, locked in that empty stare of void... but her eyes... her eyes smiled back at me and my heart rejoiced. There she was... there was my mama.

When he laid her gently back on the bed, she touched his face in thanks, closed her eyes and finally fell asleep. I watched my daddy, worn out, exhausted, pull a chair up to her side, lay his head down near her chest and close his eyes, finding peace in the darkness. I knew then it was time to fill out the papers for palliative care.

Princess Margret Hospital December 23, 2005

I had been driving to Princess Margret Hospital for many months. I knew the route by my hurting heart. Yet, that morning I got lost. Was it my mama's doing? Did she somehow know that I, her oldest daughter, would not have been able to watch her take her last breath? I knew by the silence, by the heavy wood door that was shut tight. Hospital doors were always open weren't they? I couldn't breathe.

As I reached for the knob, my dad opened the door, somehow knowing I was there. "É andata, è andata, è con gli angeli adesso, amore mio." "She's gone, she's gone, she's with the angels now, my love." He hugged me, I think.

I placed the miniature Christmas tree I had brought her on the window ledge next to those palliative care papers that never did get filled out; Mama loved Christmas, but I was too late. My sister sat by the bed, strangely calm. She had been there to see mama take her final breath, my daddy had been out of the room; mama's doing again? My body moved slowly, following my eyes, which finally rested on her face, so peaceful, the lines of pain gone, accenting a beauty that no evil could diminish; but too still after the erratic movements of yesterday. As I gently kissed my mama goodbye, I felt her spirit enter my heart. The tears wouldn't come until later, not wanting to accept defeat, but understanding that their comfort would be needed. If tears were truly the sounds of the soul, the silence was deafening.

Mama knew she was dying. For days she had been seeing visions of those called before her, beckoning in welcome. She called them by name, with eyes that seemed to see them clearly, as we watched frightened. She fought, willing her soul to stay in the body that was being ravaged; painlessness tempting her. What could she give us when she couldn't anymore? Deep in her heart she ached to love us, but knew that it would only be felt if she had the courage to accept her fate. She welcomed her wings all sparkly and light, and when the sun rose that day her spirit followed. Mama had been gifted with an honor - the most special one of all, a Christmas Angel she became that day.

The mall was bustling, yuletide music playing loudly above the laughter of excited children and the sounds of the registers as last minute panic was appeased by purchases; Christmas Eve. With a heart of sorrow, I searched the shops, my courage almost failing me with the sight of families gathered together in the food court, sipping hot chocolate, grandparents wiping sticky candy cane from young ones faces. Then I found it, the perfect gift for my mama. She had wept quietly but bravely as her beautiful curls became patches of bare. I wanted her to look beautiful on her farewell day. Her casket soft with silky pink satin, the outfit she had picked weeks ago a pretty emerald green. The hat, too, was green and soft as a cloud, a red bow adorning it. She would look like a present under a tree; our gift to the heavens my mama would be. I remember vaguely someone asking if I needed help, I explained I had found what I was looking for, and as I told her about mama and her hat, her smile faded in confusion, murmuring excuses to get away. No one wanted to deal with sadness on Christmas. Because tinsel doesn't sparkle when it's draped around death. Fuck Cancer.

I remember sitting in the parlor (stupid fancy name for a place of sorrow) of the funeral home... the smell of thousands of flowers fighting for their place... watching the mourners walk up to mama to give their last respects. I remember thinking how lovely the Christmas hat looked, her lips adorned with her favorite pink lipstick. I overheard them whispering in stunned voices, heads shaking in disbelief, saying horrible things, like she didn't resemble the Apollonia they knew... that she looked terrible... what a shame... that cancer had destroyed the beauty that she was... I knew they weren't words for my ears, but I heard... and I was angry... screaming inside... what are you saying? She's beautiful! She's still beautiful! Can't you see?? What are you saying?? Stop!! What the fuck are you saying?? Look in her eyes! Her warm brown eyes... her eyes will show you... she's still there... but her eyes would no longer open... so I silently screamed until I couldn't anymore... and then I cried.

Pine Hills Cemetery December 29, 2005

It was a gloomy day, so bitterly cold the steam rose from faces wet with tears and snowflakes falling from the heavens. The haunting melody of 'Ave Maria' lingering in our minds, her favorite song, played in the church as her last request. Apollonia's final resting place, surrounding by loved ones confused with the acceptance that she was at peace blended with sorrow that she was here no more.

Her grandchildren stood silently, holding their gifts to her; Jesse had picked a rosary created from flowers, wrapped with pearls and a note that simply said 'To my Nonna. Love, your Jesse,' because there were no words to do justice to the memories swirling in his mind; two pretty bouquets adorned with glittery pink ribbon, held tightly by her granddaughters, Sabrina and Julia, too young to fully understand that this goodbye was forever; Marco had given his goalie stick to the florist, to adorn and wrap in foliage, a tribute to the many times she had set up a goalie net made of pillows and shot pucks for him to stop. As the children placed the tokens on her casket silence fell and a beautiful monarch butterfly joined the dance of the snowflakes.

The Prosecco (The Present 2018)

Putting the finishing touches on the dining room table I watched through the window as my daddy got out of his car. I knew he was coming from the cemetery; he went regularly, especially after Sunday mass like today. As I returned to the kitchen to prepare the antipasto, I heard shouts of, "Hi Nonno!" mixed with my dad's voice greeting his grandchildren. He still had an accent, a charming tribute to his past.

I carried the platters overflowing with favorites to the table; prosciutto, thinly sliced and buttery, wrapped around slices of sweet juicy melon. Bocconcini cheese, milky and soft garnished with the basil my daddy grew in his garden; olives from the trees in Greece, brought to us fresh by our Greek neighbors, salty, spicy and oily, a perfect accompaniment to the chunks of crusty bread. My daddy's homemade vino, a tradition we had all grown up with, a touch too strong for some of us, but always enjoyed when we were together, sat ready to be poured. The main dish would be lasagna, steaming hot from the oven, the corners crispy and the mozzarella stringy. Dessert would be served later; I had made it this morning, we called it Nonna cake because I had found mama's recipe, written in her elegant writing one day. A simple sponge cake she had delighted in making for her grandchildren; that I now hoped to make for mine someday.

I reached for the bottle in the small bar fridge hidden inside the vintage cabinet I had bought and had shipped over from Venice. I heard my family come crashing into the room, taking their usual spots with the enthusiasm of hunger.

My son Jesse, the firstborn grandchild, his patience and inquisitive nature absorbing the traditions revealed to him by his grandparents. His laid back dry humor mixed with the general knowledge of everything kept us all enthralled. Marco, my youngest, full of energy and fire; he protects us all with a courage that has more to do with his heart than his physical strength. Sabrina is the wild child, the dark storms of her tantrums quickly bursting with a flash of her dimples. And there was Julia my youngest niece, sparkling like a true jewel, a gem in our hearts. She didn't remember Nonna much, but could recount many tales with fondness told to her by her sister and cousins. And, finally, my sister, the one who had surprised us with her strength; with her acceptance that Mama was ready to take her last breath when the rest of us just wanted to deny.

I felt the cork give with a tiny pop, my heart echoing the sound that was customarily the prelude to a celebration. The wine I had chosen was Nino Franco Rustico Prosecco. The sparkling wine was elegant and fresh, fruity with a touch of citrus and notes of toasted almond. Like my mama. Pairing wines with the people in my life was something I had been doing for some time, the description of the wine chosen matching perfectly with their personality. The memories today would be shared with a joyousness created from years of grief. We never stop grieving, but time grants acceptance, a journey that opens our hearts so that tears can become smiles.

Before filling champagne flutes with the bubbly spirit, I paused and reflected on the chaos with affection. Laughter, raised voices, teasing; my family gathered at a table laden with foods to pay homage to the woman who still holds us together with her spirit, Apollonia.

We will toast my daddy, whose gentle strength, giving heart and fierce protectiveness clearly shows he has become the man he was meant to be that day, alone on a ship about to set sail. Together they created a legacy for all of us, one of courage, honesty, loyalty, strength, forgiveness and unconditional love.

I have to believe in a heaven, where I picture my mama to be, cooking everyone's favorite food, snacking on sweets all day long as she loved to do, playing with children, and helping those in need. The skies are pink and the clouds marshmallow fluff. If there is a heaven this is how I want it to be, the colors of the rainbow like the colors of my mama's heart. But the most important thing would be ... that she is cancer free.

So when we feel the wispy touch of an angel's wings, the flutter of a monarch butterfly and the scent of the forget me not, like the legend of long ago, we remember...non ti scordar di mé...and we never will mama...we never will.

Lucia Colangelo is the two time #1 International Bestselling author of the inspirational 'My Vintage Collection' found in The Sisterhood folios Live Out Loud and the dark 'The Venetian Mask' from The Sisterhood folios Born To Be Me. This is the third story in the trilogy.

Lucia writes with passion and creativity; her love for words expressed in the images she creates in the minds of her readers. Her unique style continues to capture the imagination. When she's not writing she enjoys traveling, reading, gourmet pizza, pasta, lattes and wine.

Lauren Dickson

Letting the Reins Loose: The Art of Letting Go

Have you ever taken that deep dive when your brain won't shut down in bed at night? Have you pondered in the dark and silence all of the events, struggles, laughter, and tears that have brought you to exactly where you are in your life today? To have quiet reflection after all of the hustle and bustle of daily life gives an interesting perspective on life's journey. It sets us up to refocus and set a new path if we don't like our present course.

I love how looking out the window at the stars makes my heart smile; how just the tune of a song brings back a flood of memories, and all the sentimental feelings attached. Then there is the looking back on the struggles and curve balls that life so forcefully has thrown at me; and chuckling at the things I once thought I longed for, which turned out to be not right for me at all. Sometimes I felt like I was caught in between all I wished for and all I actually needed. There were things I wanted, or at least thought I wanted, and would feel hurt, angry, and frustrated when it would slip through my fingertips.

"Remember that sometimes not getting what you want
is a wonderful stroke of luck."
~Dalai Lama

I think I felt like the more I held on and tried to gain success in every area of my life, the stronger I was... but the truth is the real strength is in letting go. Letting go does not mean giving up; but rather allowing space for what is meant to be to come in. There was a long time that I struggled with so much anxiety of how my life would turn out; worrying and stressing about things that were out of my control, and fighting vigorously to keep some sort of grasp on each aspect of my life. I thought the more I tried, the more I cared, the better it would turn out. Wrong! Have you ever tried to hold sand in the grasp of your fists? It all just going to seep through anyway!

"The tighter you squeeze, the less you have."
~Thomas Merton

For a long period of time, every aspect of my life seemed to have gone awry all at the same time! Everything from promised jobs that didn't fit, to friends whose intentions weren't true, to meeting a bunch of 'frogs' before finding a 'prince', to home life; you name it. I couldn't figure out why life was being so cruel and unfair to me. In previous writing projects I expressed my journey through the heartache, pain, and lessons learned of my so-called love life, and struggles with depression. As the deep, old soul that I am, I started re-evaluating my own choices, mindset, and overall outlook on life.

So many people become so angry when life gives you obstacles; and they lose faith and hope - in God, in life, and in themselves. However, if life is constantly sending you those obstacles, signs, and lessons, it clearly wants so desperately to show you something! So, instead of becoming angry and miserable, one should look to themselves to see what they can change about their own mistakes, and decision-making. I have witnessed it, with a couple of people close to me; they continue to live their life the same way, making the same mistakes, and never learning the incredible lessons that life is trying to teach. It is sad, and frankly annoying, to see people constantly complain about life, when they flat-out refuse to learn and grow! There are so many things that are out of our control in life, and we cannot do anything about that.

We can, however, control the way we respond to what life throws our way... and that is HUGE!! Trust me, life has a better way of showing up for you, when you have a better, more positive way of reacting to the ups and downs of this remarkable journey.

I would have to say that a big turning point in me letting go of stress, expectations, and the sense of trying to control what we cannot control, was a trip I took to Newfoundland in June 2016. I went to visit my younger sister. I had spent summers there when I was a child, and they are some of the best memories of my life! It's a different atmosphere there, the east-coast vibe; breathing in that fresh air, and staring out at the vast expanse of the ocean truly gives you an extraordinarily amazing perspective on... well, everything really. It really makes you think about how large life is, and, just like the waves and tides of the ocean, that your life can change in the blink of an eye.

It was not long after I came back from that trip that someone whom I had been dating had exited my life. With all of the changes happening, I knew I had to try a new approach in the attempt to let go of all the pain, fears, and expectations of how I thought my life should go. It was November of 2016 that I started talking to a Life Coach. He is my age, 28-years-old, yet with so much wisdom and insight on the process of changing yourself to change your life. He helped me to realize some flaws in how I was handling the messiness that life can often be, and on how I was reacting to the behavior of others toward me. It was so incredibly eye-opening to have better clarity on just how liberating it is to truly not bear the weight of the world on your shoulders. I saw more clearly that by changing my approach can, and will, indeed, result in life giving back what you are giving. There was a period in my life where I wasn't sure I believed in the saying, "You get what you give." I had, for so long, given my all - given too much at times - and felt no reciprocation from others or from life in general. When truth be told, I was trying too hard, and I was getting back some of the pressure I was giving.

I started reading books like The Wisdom of the Enneagram by Don Richard Riso, and A Path with Heart by Jack Kornfield, which allowed me to understand more about my personality type, as well as spiritual and psychological growth. I have learned to have full acceptance of myself. To celebrate the utmost joy of just being alive; embracing all God has planned for my life, and being who I am. It does not mean embracing bad habits, but rather loving me fully in order to accept the pain and struggles I will face, and being in the here and now as a whole human being.

I have learned that life is our greatest teacher. I know that to be present in each moment of each day, and with each experience, is exactly what will lead to learning the most from each situation. Life will keep sending you the same message and forcing the same lessons over and over again if it has to, until we actually learn what is needed. People often focus too much on what is going wrong in their life instead of focusing on what is right. Life is often not as bad as it seems, and by accepting the lessons and applying that to how we live our lives on a daily basis, it will help move things along more freely. If you feel like you are going in circles, it is probably because you keep making the same mistakes again and again, and expecting a different result.

Part of what I love about myself, and my strength, is that I never stop discovering more about myself, and the inner workings of my mind, heart, and soul. I love to have alone time sometimes; it's crucial in making yourself whole, regardless of who or what may or may not be in your life at any given time. Some people are afraid to be alone; like they are too scared of thinking too much, or feeling too much, or actually having to face and deal with their own emotions. I have known people who think that they don't have a life unless they have a significant other, or possess certain materialistic items that they think will make them happy. They don't know where to even begin when it comes to loving themselves or living a full life on their own. I have learned to never fully trust someone unless I know they see me for who I really am, and would fight for me, and be willing to knock down the walls that I had to figuratively build to protect my heart.

"Only trust someone who can see these three things in you:
the sorrow behind your smile, the love behind your anger,
and the reason behind your silence."
~Unknown

I came to a decision that I would not date for a while. I had only met fake, selfish, immature guys, who didn't even know themselves enough or what they wanted, so I was better off flying solo for a time. I didn't want to be one of those people who are so fixated on 'finding' their life mate. Sometimes the harder you search for something, the more you will miss the important things that are there waiting for you to see them. I was living my life, and determined to fulfill every creative passion and goal of mine. The more excited I am about my own little world, so to speak, the more attractive I felt anyway. I was living my life, and letting the rest happen when it was meant to. Now, I have an amazing boyfriend of six months, whom I met completely out of the blue. When I wasn't looking, life brought me something and someone like no other I had experienced before. Two people, who were living their lives for themselves, and not up to someone else's standards, and life saw a good fit. Perhaps everything life knew I needed and was waiting for that right time to present it to me. It is true what they say, that things happen when you least expect it. Let love find you... it will if you want it to, and are open to it. Life has a funny way of working out.

"Well, life has a funny way of sneaking up on you when you
think everything's okay and everything's going right.
And life has a funny way of helping you out when you think
everything's gone wrong and everything blows up in your face."
~Alanis Morissette, Ironic

In this process of letting go, however, there is one thing that I have had a hard time letting go of; my up and down relationship with my mother. She means the world to me, and I love her dearly, but it is true what is said about mothers and daughters. Statistics show the strain on the bonds between mothers and daughters. For years, I have bent over backwards for my Mom, and it often goes unappreciated, or ignored altogether. I live my life well; am very mature, responsible, and make good choices for myself. Yet, I often have found that she never truly sees me. I yearn for satisfying conversations and a pleasant relationship with her. Sometimes it's great, but more often than not, it seems as though my efforts are a waste of time; trying to break the cycle of a misunderstanding, or me not being able to get a word in edgewise. Or how, in a split second, a simple, upbeat conversation can suddenly turn amiable chit chats into angry or painful ones. When things are good, they're good; but when things are not good between us, it hurts me to my core. Some days I think, forget it, I'm done trying. Then others, I find it so hard to let this go... because she's my Mom. If your Mother doesn't see all that you are, is there much hope for someone else to see, you know? I know I cannot control other people, or their actions, and I know that if others do not appreciate the woman that I am, it is an issue within them and not me. No one should have to drain themselves dry from trying so hard to gain the respect of others. It should be given more freely than that. I am completely understanding and sympathetic of everything my Mom has been through. That is why I look out for her like I do, to take care of her. I don't want her living with regrets, just like I don't want that for myself. Like me, my Mom has a big heart, and also like me, she often has cared too much; which is why I have tried to show her what I have learned that has helped me in ways I will always be grateful for.

I know who I am; I'm not perfect, no one is, but I love myself, in all my glory, and my flaws. I choose to never stop learning and growing. We are all works in progress, but a beautiful work of art at the same time!

The fear of the unknown is something that haunts some people daily. I have my never-failing faith in God, which keeps me strong. I may not always understand His plan, but I know he's got me. The unknown in life used to frighten me; not knowing what's going to happen or when; but now it actually excites me. I don't dwell on the past (although some days it would be nice to go back to the 'good ol' days'). I don't worry about the future either. I make the most of right now, because that is exactly what is going to get me to my future. By worrying about the unknown, we keep ourselves from seeing the bigger picture. You would fail to see the little, beautifully spectacular moments that sneak up on you, because of the desperate want to somehow control what has yet to come.

That feeling of just letting go is so incredibly liberating! I know that as long as I do my part, the rest will work itself out. I am so grateful for my job which I have worked so hard for, my family and loved ones, and my knowing that I don't know what I don't know. I look at even the simplest things now, and see the gorgeous ambiance and beauty; in the light of the sun, the wind in the trees, the laughter of children, the stillness before dawn, as if the world was almost perfect.

I still have days of feeling that anxious butterfly in my stomach, and not even knowing why. However, now I don't let it consume my every thought and take over my days. I am constantly working on knowing myself better, which helps me live a much better and healthier lifestyle. I am proud of my accomplishments, and am gentle with myself for my shortcomings. The life I want can be achieved.

It would be extremely boring if we could plan every moment of our lives. There is so much excitement in knowing that a new friend or an incredible opportunity could surprise me at any time.

Life is like a highway; the roads or exits that you almost took, the paths you chose to follow, and the roads which have yet to be built. Thinking back on the places I might have turned, and thanking God that he re-directed me to better places. I don't need a destination to take that first step; and when it comes to my life, the journey is indeed the destination. There's always more to discover and explore, and that is what makes life so magical!

I have never really liked the question, "Where do you see yourself in five years?" I have my hopes and dreams, but life has its own timing. Not being where I think I hope to be could actually be a great thing. Life definitely has more in store than I could even comprehend at this point, and that is alright with me.

"Do not let the fire go out, spark by irreplaceable spark
in the hopeless swamps of the not-quite, the not-yet,
and the not-at-all.
Do not let the hero in your soul perish in lonely frustration
for the life you deserved and have never been able to reach.
The world you desire can be won.
It exists, it is real, it is possible... It's yours."
~Ayn Rand, Atlas Shrugged

Lauren Dickson, WPIC Certified Wedding & Events Coordinator, Co-Author of two #1 International Bestsellers (The Sisterhood Folios: Live Out Loud, and Born To Be Me), and an all-around creative, old soul. Through her struggles and heartache, she has built self-resiliency and a deeper connection and love for herself and with life. It is through her own experiences and compassionate demeanor that she hopes to impact and inspire others to fight their demons, discover their authentic individuality, and fully embrace life, not just survive it.

Sonia Dolar

LIttle Warrior

Not a Typical Saturday

I arrived home to a locked door. All day I had been worried. Our family rule was to phone and check in. I had stopped at a retail store to borrow a phone, and tried calling from my friend, Sandra's house, too. There was no answer. Shouldn't someone be home worrying about me? My mother would worry about where I was if I did not call, because someone should always know where a 10-year-old is, but no one was worried today. My regular Saturday routine was to swim at the YMCA with my friend. We weren't competitive swimmers - not even really very athletic, but it was a weekend ritual followed by much more exciting things like lunch and shopping. I was always independent, as I liked to arrange my own activities and be out all day, but a check-in, in the afternoon was standard.

There was a message for me taped to the door of my house to go and see the neighbor. I not only came home to a house with no lights on, no noise, but it was locked up - and locked up good, even the screen door was locked. My 10-year-old imagination kicked in. Were they off doing something fun without me? Was my brother being favored with special time with my parents? My thoughts were racing... did they leave the country without me? I didn't want to live at my neighbors. I'm not even sure if I liked them!

I had been out all day; I was tired and I was hungry. I forced myself to walk next door. The hollow rap on the door matched the hollow feeling in my stomach. Mrs. Redwood opened the door to what I just knew was bad news. Through tight lips and a forced smile she told me my father and brother were in a terrible accident. My mother had been called at home and was with them at the hospital. My father was about to go into surgery. And she left me there. No hug, no cup of cocoa; nothing. I don't remember anything else that happened at her house. I have a vivid memory of most things in my life. But not this time. I've heard that in times of trauma you often block things out. My nervous system must have kicked in to protect me from the rush of emotions: fear, guilt, worry, anger, sorrow.

The next thing I remember was sitting in my dad's room in the hospital. He was in intensive care. I remember some conversations, the beep of machines. I remember being so afraid. My father's motorcycle had been hit by a senior driver who didn't see him. My brother was fortunate to have been thrown from the bike, but my father's body had been crushed on impact. He was beyond injured; he was broken. His leg had been ripped open, he lost his knee cap, and also had his arm and hand on that same side of his body badly damage. Everything required surgery. Multiple surgeries.

Unexpected Warriors

My mother, my brother, and I were on another journey. When a health crisis, hits survival kicks in. Following the immediate shock you work on adrenaline. Energy is high as you put all the changes into action. I think that's why I don't remember a lot from the early days. It was just pure survival mode. But when you eventually settle into routine and see the extended timeline of recovery uneasiness, fear and anxiety take over. People help you with things that need to get done. They bring your food, your house is managed, and the bills get paid in the beginning, but this, too, wanes.

Our whole schedule changed. Even though my dad was in the hospital, and we were most compassionate for his circumstances, we were all affected. We had a visiting schedule at the hospital. It impacted my homework, and my free time. We met with doctors, nurses, learned about medical equipment – the lights, the monitors, the beeping – and what they all meant. We watched and prayed as his body was slowly rebuilt with multiple surgeries and difficult physiotherapy. The hospital became my home; the roommates of my father became my friends.

Our local church and community were very supportive with many people reaching out sending cards, flowers and meals. But I needed so much more. Each surgery brought anxiety not knowing what the outcome would be, what kind of injuries would persist, what his future would be like, what would mine be like? And what if the operation was not successful? What if there was a complication and we lost him? Watching my strength and the pillar of our family lying in a bed, helpless and inactive, and not speaking, brought fear and trepidation, and I felt compelled to look for strength somewhere. I sought out mentors.

I found comfort in music, and support from my pastor and music community. The hospital also became a second home and I learned to speak up and ask many questions of staff. I found a hunger to learn; maybe my piano adjudicator, the nurse, doctors, another patient, a teacher, maybe even a perfect stranger, I always thought that there was a potential from learning from different people and conversations that I had.

My brother found ways to cope, as well. He had some counseling but still has trouble talking about the accident. That leaves me feeling like there is still a lot he hasn't processed. We were all a great support, though, to one another. It's easy to become exhausted because you are between two homes – your own and the hospital. Emotions turn from worry to sadness because, although the condition may be improving, the timeline seems unending. It's easy to neglect your own health. The empathy for your loved one and other family members may grow thin, help with meals and other things around your home eases off, and you wonder if you can survive it all. The hard reality is that family caregivers are under-recognized and under-supported. But we persevered and held each other up.

Life is precious; it needs to be enjoyed, savored, and shared. I was fortunate to enjoy that bonding experience with my brother and mother, and understand the fragility of life at an early age. I think I have a higher appreciation for my parents than most, and learned to appreciate my own ability to get through trials, and what I need to manifest my future. Your family can become closer, or be ripped apart financially and emotionally during these times of crisis.

Warrior Mom

My mother, understanding our stress, and feeling her own uncertain future enrolled us in Transcendental Meditation with the very same Maharishi Yogi who coached The Beatles. This led to many other experiences, and my openness for 'different' and 'alternative' learning started early.

My family was very fortunate that my parents had saved for such an emergency, and, although I remember hearing, "No," a lot to wants, there was a commitment to food, our home, lessons and education. Luckily my mother was a good leader and she cared for us well. She was disciplined about expenses and allocation of money. And she taught me well. I was included in the conversations about bill paying, property taxes, and filing income tax returns. This made me very financially responsible in my adult life.

She endured years of an uncertain future. She was a single mom; but she wasn't. She was so committed to my father and his recovery. But she never neglected us. How she did it all is still a mystery to me.

"A woman is like a teabag; you never know how strong it is until you put it in hot water."
~Eleanor Roosevelt

I learned from my mom that her tenacity had developed in her own childhood. Growing up during WWII many things were just not available; they had very little, and often had to go barefoot, relying on the Red Cross for basic necessities. I modeled a lot of my mom's traits, like my affinity for finance. But I wrote my own story when it comes to shoes; I can't live with less than 50 pairs!

Warrior Dad

One of the few vivid memories I have from the hospital is sitting in my dad's room. The nurse explained the equipment a little bit and had me look at a monitor with her. "Yes, I will keep my eye on his heart monitor, and press the buzzer immediately if the line changes," I told her. This is what she instructed me to do right away when I arrived for my visit because he had developed blood clots. What an abrupt realization that my father, though still young, could have health complications due to his inactive lifestyle. I watched my father's heart monitor flat line; did I press the buzzer? There was so much noise, a flurry of activity from the nurses, loud voices. I was paralyzed with fear. What a responsibility for such a young girl.

He had experienced a blood clot passing through his heart. Right in front of me. But he was a fighter. He fought through those many years of physical rebuilding. He also fought through a tough life, having lost both his parents at the age of four, and then escaped communist rule in his country. We were scheduled to return there on a family trip, but his accident prevented that. Perhaps there was a reason we were not supposed to return.

Growing up an orphan he wanted to teach me early on to stand on my own two feet with lessons in mathematics, philosophy, and other life skills. This led to that brave independence I already had at just 10 years of age; and continued to serve me well when I had to grow up so quickly on that Saturday arriving home to a locked and empty house.

"Now, consider that you only have one mind and one body. Prepare them for life, care for them. You can enhance your mind over time. A person's main asset is themselves, so preserve and enhance yourself. The most important investment that you can make is in yourself."
~Warren Buffett

With Gratitude

My music was such a great source of joy to me. I worked playing piano at a local hotel from the age of fifteen until I went to University. I loved to get dressed up and be the center of attention. But I also was so grateful each day for the simple things like the fresh cut flowers on the baby grand, and to hear how perfectly tuned it was. It is quite something to have a career, or even make some part-time income from something that brings you such joy.

My inquisitive mind allowed me to meet many people and learn so much through music. I think this stemmed from my time in the hospital with my father. I would never allow myself to be bored; I always had books to read, and struck up conversations with the doctors and nurses when visiting my dad. I still travel, now, with more books than I have time to read just to be sure I don't run out! I met many professional musicians, athletes, photographers, and business executives while playing piano. I was eager to learn about their work and their lives, and was richer for having an open mind to listen to their stories.

I remember meeting the Maharishi Yogi dressed in his long white chemise and long hair. We all learned about mental focus and relaxation techniques. And this enabled all of us to manage stress and work in congruence with each other and the hospital to heal ourselves– and my dad. This encouraged me to learn other techniques, and introduced me to numerous other authorities, like Dr. John Grey.

Spending so much time in the hospital with my dad gave me more empathy for other people, learning about people and their conditions and situations. I met many families who traveled to Canada for health care because they could not get the same care in their own country. I am proud to be a Canadian and forever grateful for the access to healthcare that many people do not have around the world.

"Be thankful for what you have: you'll end up having more,
if you concentrate on what you don't have you will never,
ever have enough."
~Oprah Winfrey

Warrior On

Community is such an important part of life. I love seeing the 'Senior Mafia' in the local McDonald's where I live. There is one lady with matching clothes and jewelry who seems to be the organizer. It is a tight-knit Greek community and it makes me laugh because they take over the whole place. But it keeps them all active, vital, and connected; as it did for me when I didn't want to feel alone.

There were times when community felt too intrusive. We grew up in the Catholic Church, and often I felt kind of embarrassed because I didn't like to be mentioned publicly or be noticed. Everyone knew that my dad was sick, and money was tight. I felt they looked at us with pity or disdain, and always felt we were the topic of conversation in some way. I think now of being scrutinized by people more than they actually do as a result. But the church also rallied around us and helped.

My pastor specifically opened up a whole new world to me through music. He took me to my very first public performance and he asked me on the way home if I would like to accompany him to go and visit some sick and elderly people. I played for an elderly woman. I remember her barely being able to speak. But I brought her joy just by playing a few songs for her. My music was quickly more than just about me. I volunteered my time often playing piano. Many people could cook, or organize events; I could play. I could express emotion through classical piano. I felt it as I played and translated it to the listening audience. I especially enjoyed playing opera music. I could feel all the drama through the loud and soft tones; the love scenes and tragedies conveyed through my fingers. I think I especially resonated with the sadness when I played in nursing homes because of the fragility of life I had known since my childhood.

I loved playing in small festival and competitions, but through Father Charles, who was an avid musician himself, I learned to give back to the community, too. And since he was a missionary that traveled the world he opened my eyes to his international world and his gift of giving. I was the recipient of his stamp collection from all the letters that he received from those whose lives he had touched and inspired around the world. With the church I played Christmas cantatas, and I continued to volunteer playing piano at senior's residences for many years.

Music may never have developed for me in the way it did if I didn't have the need to seek out mentors, or have an outlet for my grief and worry. I have been so fortunate to have many mentors, and to have met so many fascinating people, like jazz great Trombone Shorty, and even an opportunity to study with Oscar Peterson. I had to decline that for my university studies, but consider myself so privileged just to have had the chance.

I learned to depend on myself and believe in myself. The bridges that I built through my various relationships created a path for my future. I will always take a chance to meet someone, or experience something new. I always want to know the 'who, what, and why' of things. I feel that I always want to leave the door open for an opportunity. I have been so blessed by the lessons life taught me, and the possibilities that mentors helped to inspire in me.

"The way to develop the Best that is in a person is by appreciation and encouragement."
~Charles Schwab

And I learned perseverance and hard work from both of my parents. My career in finance is most likely a direct result of having an understanding and appreciation for money from watching my mother handle our affairs. And my positive attitude has to come from my dad. He endured so much, but never gave up. I grew up with these two warriors as my guides.

That observant young girl who grew up so fast still lives within me. She is the student always ready to ask and learn. She is adventurous and social, not afraid to meet new people and hear their stories. She is the volunteer who knows the value of giving back to community that supported her. She is my little warrior.

Sonia Dolar is a Canadian, Living in Toronto; Born in 1965; Tail end baby boomer; York University; Chartered Financial Planner; member of Elder Planner Studies; speaker, author of the upcoming books
The Women's Guide to Entrepreneurship, Top 10 strategies for She Commerce and Women Think Business– The Balancing Act

I am a woman of strength.
Nothing can break my spirit.
I am wild and free. I am a warrior of light.
I AM ME.
~ Lynn Titton

Eileen Giudice

From Fear to Faith

When I reflect back on the last twelve years of my life, I can see how it's been a process of not only birthing my inner warrior, but also meeting her face to face. It has also become clear to me that growing up in the city of Camden, New Jersey provided the fertile soil for those seeds to be planted.

Despite being an only child for 8 1/2 years, I had a large extended family. I have fond memories of growing up playing with my cousins. We played often right outside on the city streets. We were carefree. We knew it was time to go home when we saw the street lights come on. There were no cell phones or pagers. We used to jump double dutch, play tag, kick ball, dodge ball, and stick ball. We also enjoyed games like 1-2-3 red light, o'clock, hopscotch, and hide and seek. We would ride bikes to the nearby city park, riding 'shotgun' on the handle bars with a friend when we didn't have our own ride. We would also ride two per swing, one sitting and the other standing. Fun and crazy times we had for sure! No helmets, no seatbelts, no playground rules. That was life growing up in the seventies.

Being raised in a Puerto Rican household, I learned the importance of family, respect for others, and pride in my culture. Just about everything I experienced was saturated with flavor and passion. The way our food waras prepared, the music we listened to and danced to, and the way we communicated with each other. Even though I was surrounded by a loving family, there was a part of me that felt alone. I never felt like I truly fit in anywhere. I never felt truly SEEN and HEARD. Many times I would express thoughts to others and they would look at me like I was crazy. I started to feel like maybe there was something wrong with me. I seemed to always see, hear, and feel things much deeper than those around me. I didn't know any other way. This created a sense of fear inside of me. I felt I was unusual. Because of this, I didn't want to stand out and be different. I was afraid I wouldn't be accepted by others. It certainly didn't help that I had a skin condition called eczema that, at times, would be extremely uncomfortable and visible on the surface. People would stare, kids would make nasty comments and this caused me to become very embarrassed and self-conscious. This reinforced my belief that it was not safe to be ME. I felt that I had to cover up; I didn't want to be seen.

Since I didn't feel as though I fit in anywhere, I developed the ability to blend in everywhere. I became somewhat of a chameleon. "Am I wearing stripes or polka dots today?" "Is my color bright or dim?" You get the idea. I saw this as a real strength. I was able to shape-shift to accommodate just about any situation I found myself in. Looking back on it now, I see that it was a survival strategy. I thought that in order to be LIKED by others, I had to be LIKE them. I wrote a poem about how I felt when I was in second grade.

Alone

How sad it is to be alone when no one else is there
You feel so left out, that words cannot compare
It's an awful feeling that gets you deep inside
Which makes you feel so lonely
You have no place to hide.

When I read this now, I can hear my soul speaking, expressing a deep wisdom. We are all on this journey together, but we must all walk our own path.

I lived in the city of Camden until the end of my eighth grade year. During that time I attended Catholic school. I had to wear a uniform, and was often teased and harassed walking home from school. Because of this, I started to bring a change of clothes with me to school so that when I walked home, I would 'blend' in more and be less of a target. However, one day while walking home I got the sense I was being followed. I could see the boy in my peripheral vision on the other side of the street. He then crossed to my side, and I in turn crossed to the other side, trying to avoid him. Suddenly, I felt a lot of pressure up against my low back. I thought he had a gun at my back. I kept walking quickly and I don't remember his exact words, but they sounded sexual in nature. I was TERRIFIED!!! It all happened so quickly, but all I can remember was that a fire rose up inside of me and I burst out screaming, cursing, swinging, and bringing as much attention as I could to the situation. Suddenly he ran away because people started to open their windows and doors to see what all the commotion was about. After that, the only thing I remember was running like the wind, or as we would say 'booking' all the way home! I got inside, locked the door, and tried to catch my breath. Complete, primal fear was what I felt. Oddly enough, I never shared that experience with anyone. I just buried the fear and pain. Although I didn't realize it at the time, I experienced the first glimpse of my Inner Warrior.

Fast forward to the year 2001, when on May 12, I became fortunate enough to marry my soul mate, Victor. It was an exciting time and we were looking forward to starting a family right away. Little did we know the bittersweet journey that lay ahead of us. Between July 2002 and April 2003 we experienced three miscarriages. One of which required me to have emergency surgery due to it being an ectopic pregnancy. As if that wasn't enough, Vic's mom passed away suddenly in January 2003 and in May 2003 I was laid off from my job!! Suffice it to say, I was physically and emotionally burnt out. Our marriage was tested from the very beginning. We both sought out counseling and slowly began moving forward in our journey together. It's been said that, "Experiences along the path can either make or break you." We were determined to believe that all of these things were helping to establish a rock solid foundation for our marriage. We grew stronger together with every tear we shed.

In July 2003, I began a Physical Therapy position at an insurance company doing utilization review. It was a nice change from the clinical settings that I had worked in up to that point. I would review cases and make a determination of frequency and duration of skilled care based on the clinical information that was sent in. I really enjoyed it and things all seemed to be falling back into some semblance of normal. We had taken our focus off of having children, and much to our pleasant surprise, I found out I was pregnant in October 2003. Of course I didn't really start enjoying and settling into the pregnancy until almost 5 months along. The fear of miscarriage was still fresh in my mind. When I found myself finally able to 'exhale', I truly cherished the remaining months of my pregnancy.

My due date was set for June 21, 2004; however, Alexander Luis Giudice decided he would make his grand entrance at 4:32 a.m. on June 16, 2004. I call it a 'grand' entrance because there was a severe thunderstorm while I was in labor. So much so, that the lights went out in the hospital and my father was in a car accident right outside the hospital on his way to see us. I was on one floor in labor and delivery, and he was on another getting x-rays and CAT Scans! It was a comedy of errors for sure. To make things even more interesting, I found out that Hurricane Alex was the first named storm, and the first major hurricane of the 2004 hurricane season!!

I should mention here that the name Alexander came to me in a dream, before I even knew the sex of the baby... coincidence, I think not. I think what we call coincidence is just God's way of winking at us. I believe that everything we experience is divinely timed, ordered, and organized. Often times these events appear as chaos, making NO sense whatsoever. However, there IS a Master Plan in process. Neither our eyes nor our brain are wired to see and understand these things. This is where our 'eyes of faith' are required. 'We walk by faith, not by sight.' There is no logic associated with faith. Faith arises in the absence of logic and understanding.

So there he was a 7 lb. 6 oz. bundle of deliciousness! A full head of dark brown hair, mesmerizing brown eyes, and a scent that was divine. My heart was overflowing! Up until that point in my life, I had never experienced such an opening in my heart. It was so overwhelming that it frequently brought me to tears. It was, and still is, such a different kind of love. It is very difficult to put into words. It is an experience like no other. And so began a new chapter in our lives, we were now proud parents of a beautiful baby boy.

After about a year or so, we discussed the possibility of having another child. We wanted a playmate for Alexander, but more importantly, I had a deep sense that our family was not yet complete. From a fertility standpoint, I wasn't getting any younger and my biological clock was ticking LOUDLY! Of course we started out with the fun, traditional method of getting pregnant. However, after a good 6-8 months, we had no luck. I was already pushing 40, so we decided to consult with a reproductive endocrinologist. I had bloodwork and various standard tests performed. Soon after began the discussion about the possibility of fertility treatments. Although I was grateful that there were a variety of options to explore, I was disappointed that we were walking down this road. I was determined to move forward with these treatments because I felt that our family circle was not yet complete. So it began; the journey on the unpredictable fertility treatment highway! Methodically timed patches, oral and injectable hormones, multiple doctor appointments, tests, etc. Ughhh!!!!!

Meanwhile trying to balance my roles as a full time Home Care Physical Therapist, mommy, and wife, this was not an easy task. But my faith, strength of spirit, and support from family and friends helped to maintain my sanity. "There, but for the Grace of God, went I." Days turned into months and months turned into years. All together we went through 3 intrauterine inseminations (IUIs) and 3 in vitro fertilization (IVF) cycles with NO success. We also had some medically indicated rest periods in between as well. I shed many tears, battled mood swings, and expressed a lot of frustration to anyone that would listen. During this time my husband and I attended a couples infertility support group so that we had a place to safely share our feelings with others who knew exactly what we were going through. Although we were both on this journey together, we experienced and expressed our thoughts about it completely different. I knew we had so much more love to offer another child and I wondered why this had to be so difficult for us. It also didn't help that during this time everyone else around me seemed to get and stay pregnant so easily. My depression and anxiety were at an all-time high. All we wanted was ONE more child so that our Alexander would have a sibling. Was this too much to ask?

In the fall of 2008, I started seeing an acupuncturist who specialized in women dealing with infertility issues. I had experienced acupuncture in the past for various reasons, and found it to be extremely helpful. This acupuncturist would treat women dealing with general infertility, and also those specifically going through in vitro fertilization. He would be with you the day the embryos were ready to be transferred into your uterus and do a pre and post transfer treatment. At this point, we were open to trying ANYTHING to increase our chances of success. The doctor recommended placing 2 embryos in to help increase the chances of at least one being successfully implanted. Several weeks passed and the day came for our first ultrasound. It was early December of 2008 and much to our surprise, there were two heartbeats! Both of the embryos successfully implanted and we couldn't have been more thrilled. Finally, all of the time, effort, injections, alternative therapies, tears, money spent, had paid off! The doctors follow you very closely in the beginning with frequent bloodwork and ultrasounds. At one of those appointments, the doctor was doing his routine checkup and started to perform the ultrasound. I was looking at the screen, but it was all a blur to me. The doctor was quiet for what seemed like an eternity. My first thought was "OMG, maybe he doesn't see the heartbeats and he's trying to figure out how to tell me! Maybe I had another miscarriage!" He shook me from my thoughts when he said, "Very interesting." I responded with, "What?" He replied, "Don't worry, nothing is wrong, it's just that now there are 3 heartbeats." "You're kidding me, right?" He said, "NOPE!" Evidently, one of the embryos split and became identical twins. So, now I had a singleton and an identical twin pregnancy at the same time! This was definitely much more than we bargained for.

Any multiple-pregnancy is considered high risk, but the identical twins inside of me were sharing a placenta. That in itself was risky due to the possibility of an imbalance of nutrient distribution. Often times, one baby can take more nutrition from the placenta, which may cause the other baby to become severely malnourished, or even die in utero.

Due to the high risk nature of my pregnancy, the doctor recommended that we consider reduction. This is the process by which, under ultrasound guidance, they insert a needle into the amniotic sac with a medication that STOPS the baby's heartbeat. I thought, "There is no way! We've spent the last couple of years trying to have another child, going through multiple fertility treatments, disappointments, tears, money spent, and now we are being put into a position to decide whether or not we are essentially killing one of our babies???!!" I was MORTIFIED! To make things even worse, the higher risk identical twins would be the ones that would have to be reduced. We just couldn't wrap our minds around this and we were extremely uncomfortable making this decision. The doctor said we had plenty of time to discuss it. Looking back now, I know that the doctor was looking out for my overall health. After all, we set out with the intention of only having one more child!

After a lot of prayer and soul searching, Vic and I decided that we would move forward with the doctor's recommendation of reduction, ultimately, for the sake of my own health. He was a highly skilled and respected doctor in his field and we trusted his advice. In total we endured three attempts at this reduction process. Ultimately, the doctor was unable to perform the procedure. The placenta of the singleton was wrapped around the twins. I'll never forget what the nurse said. "Someone else made your reduction decision." I immediately knew that she was referring to God. Although the idea of having triplets was daunting, we were grateful that the decision was taken out of our hands.

On April 2, 2009, due to a bleeding incident, I was hospitalized and placed on complete bed-rest for the remainder of my pregnancy. During this time, I was being monitored very closely. Unfortunately, on April 21, 2009 at 23 weeks I went into labor due to an infection that developed in my uterus. So with no medication and the Grace of God, I gave birth to my three angels: Isabella Madeline, Lucas Alan, and Victor Thomas. Although I was devastated at the loss, there was a beautiful feeling of peace in the room.... unable to explain, but everyone in the room felt it as well. I held each of them and had them baptized. Later that day, a friend came to visit; she hugged me and whispered in my ear, "You're a warrior." No one had ever referred to me as a warrior before, and if I was a warrior, I sure as hell felt like a defeated one! I felt smashed on all levels; physical, emotional, mental, and spiritual. The weeks and months to follow would involve IV antibiotics for me, a burial service for my angels, and a lot of grieving. God's grace was certainly carrying me through all of it.

"The deeper that sorrow carves into your being, the more joy you can contain."
~Khalil Gibran

I was determined to become better and not bitter. By September of 2009, I was back to work and moving forward the best that I could. There continued to be a fire burning inside of me that wouldn't let me give up on completing my family. People around me asked, "Aren't you afraid of going through the IVF process again and it not working out?" Hell, yes I was, but my faith became bigger than my fear. Just because you have faith, doesn't mean you don't feel fear. You definitely FEEL fear, but you MOVE forward anyway! So with Faith and Fear holding hands, I moved forward through another IVF cycle, and in March 2010, I was pregnant.

On November 24, 2010 at 9:25 am, I gave birth to Lucas Victor Giudice!! The feeling of completion was visceral and indescribable. He was, and still is, our light at the end of a long, dark tunnel.

By now, I had become increasingly aware that God was building my resumé of faith. That was a good thing, because in May of 2015, I heard the three words no one ever wants to hear, 'You have cancer'– breast cancer specifically. What? Really? I was diligent with getting my mammograms, pap smears, and self-checks. My brain had me dead, buried, and in my next lifetime. I was in a fog and disbelief. I remember going home and literally dropping first to my knees, and then I was face down on the floor saturating it with salty tears. I prayed and remember saying, "God I know you didn't bring me this far to have it end like this. I just know that you're not finished with me yet!"

This is what I heard in my spirit, "There is a death happening inside, making room for the birth of the new. There will now be a new level of strength, grace, and faith." And so I was thrust into an unknown journey that would include 3 months of chemotherapy,

2 mastectomies, and 5 times a week for 6 weeks of radiation treatment. During this time, we were fortunate to receive love and support from family, friends, and our township community. People reached out with cards, meals, and gifts of encouragement. We will forever be grateful for the outpouring of love.

One day, I forced myself to stand in front of the mirror and really LOOK at myself: NO hair, NO breasts, and broken skin. There I was, stripped of everything that I (and we, as a society) defined as beauty for a woman. Intellectually I knew that true beauty comes from within, but until you are experiencing that loss, face to face, you have no idea how you will react. I became overwhelmed with emotion, not a pity party, but more so tears of compassion. Compassion for the one who persisted and endured through all of the obstacles and disappointments that life had thrown her way. I found myself thanking God for removing the barriers that clouded my view of the truth and depth of my being. I know it doesn't sound logical, but that's the mystery of faith.

They're not called 'growing pains' for nothing. Although I had a lot of support around me, no one could walk through the fire for me. It was my path; and mine alone. I would often hear things like, 'keep fighting,' 'stay strong,' 'there is a light at the end of the tunnel'. I did believe this on some level, but I thought to myself, "I don't want to WAIT that long to experience this light." Then I had a realization that this light we wait to experience at the END of the tunnel is a light, a "Divine Spark," that we all carry inside of us. Then I heard, "The desire of Darkness is the experience of its OWN Light." I dug deep to connect with my God given light inside to help illuminate my walk (sometimes only a crawl) through this dark tunnel.

This was no easy task, and required a ton of courage. I was determined to continue dancing and standing firmly in a place of gratitude. Often times God's blessings are not in what He gives, but in what He takes away. Soon after, I became inspired to write this:

Rainbow Blessings

Blessings within, blessings without,
How can we ever be in doubt?
They are found in the sunshine,
They are found in the rain.
Deep within our joy,
And even in our pain.
Sometimes they are seen as obvious,
Most often in disguise,
But what may come to us as a big surprise,
Is that God as Master of All,
Is inviting us to answer His call,
And dare to believe that HE is deep within
All of the experiences we find ourselves in.
So then let's celebrate life from beginning to end
And slowly reveal His glorious grace within.

One day while in yoga class I became emotional while performing the Warrior 2 pose. It wasn't from physical pain; it just touched me so deeply, so much so that I had another download of inspiration...

Warrior Pose

As much as this pose demonstrates strength and stability, it is also a representation of vulnerability and humility. We have a wide stance with our arms wide open which exposes our heart. It teaches us that no matter what we face in life, our true strength and gifts lie in the courageous ability to maintain an open heart. A true warrior knows that in allowing our hearts to remain open love can flow freely in the giving and receiving. This is nurturing, strengthening, and healing for this journey of faith on earth. Love is the most powerful ammunition..... It is the eternal liberator.

After reading this, I realized that for a huge part of my life I carried a shield based on fear. The shield was over my heart and I thought

I was protecting myself from harm. I didn't want to get my hopes up too high in case of disappointment. What a set up that is! In trying to prevent myself from sorrow, I was also blocking the entrance for joy. What I've come to experience is that joy and sorrow are two sides of the same coin. You can't truly know one without the other. Today my shield of choice is Faith.

"And the day came when the risk it took to remain tight in the bud was more painful than the risk it took to blossom."
~Anais Nin

This shield of Faith has taught me that things are not happening TO me, rather FOR my highest good. This helps me to maintain an open heart and increase my capacity to receive love and healing through anything. It has also taught me that in order to be brave, you have to first feel fear. This is not weakness as long as you continue to move forward, courageously, the best you can. We are always doing the best we can; it just may vary in appearance based on what we are dealing with. Lastly, it has taught me to not fear the darkness, for there are certain things that can only be seen in the dark. Often the darkness helps you to remember your own light. You can't see the beauty of the stars, without the darkness of the sky.

I believe that we all have an Inner Warrior that has the potential to be ignited by the Divine Spark within us. It is the part of us that has grit, that never gives up, that endures, that perseveres, and that is determined to THRIVE and not just SURVIVE!!

Warrior Wisdom

To be a warrior is not to be without wounding. Instead, a warrior is one who has been wounded multiple times at the core of their being; a heart shattering so deep, that the pieces forget how to reassemble. A true warrior knows that the pieces were not meant to be recovered, but to be transformed into a new creation. They recognize this as a shattering of the prison of Ego, the box of comfort that we live in that limits our highest potential.

From the outside looking in, these beings may appear as broken, victims of circumstance. However, a warrior embraces failure as a part of success; they know that within every obstacle lies an opportunity, every breaking is followed by a blessing, and that the greatest blessings often come with the biggest burdens. They become better not bitter. They use adversity as a stepping stool to ascend higher toward their destiny. Warrior wisdom knows that true peace is not found in knowing all the answers, rather it is found in the ability to STAY with NOT knowing. They have learned the power that lies in maintaining an open heart in all experiences. They never give up and continue to say "YES" to life, for they know that what they withhold from others, they also withhold from themselves. Warriors bow to fear and pain. They have learned to gracefully tango with the shadows, for they know that shadows can only appear because of the presence of light. These beings are the ones that become the lighthouses, helping to illuminate the path for those who find themselves lost in the darkness.

Eileen Giudice earned her Masters degree in Physical Therapy from Rutgers University and The University of Medicine and Dentistry in 1991. Throughout her career, she has practiced in a variety of settings. She believes in the importance of treating the WHOLE person and not just a specific injury or diagnosis.

Since then, she received her certification as a Reiki Master and is currently working towards a certification as a Healing Touch Practioner. Eileen lives in Southern NJ with her husband and two beautiful sons. She presently works for a Home Health Agency where she helps to empower people to restore their strength, balance, and confidence in safely performing their daily functional activities.

Better to live one year as a tiger,
than a hundred as a sheep.
~ Madonna

Sholina Jivraj

Rise of The Divine Feminine: From Pain to Passion

"Some of the biggest questions of the heart unfold as a path, not an answer."
~Sholina Jivraj

"What the f*?!" I stared at the pelvic floor physiotherapist like she was levitating in the examining room. "Stage *two* pelvic organ prolapse? Diastasis Recti? That's not possible."

I was in total denial. I mean, I knew that based on the pain and pressure in my pelvic area that I had symptoms of something brewing for a while, but I didn't have incontinence. Surely that would be the biggest telltale sign that either my uterus or bladder was falling down, right? I was sure she was mistaken. I taught fitness for twenty years. I taught yoga. I did Kegels. I did high intensity training and core work that was more creative and effective than the average fitness devotee could imagine. Diastasis Recti? Hey, I had six pack abs even right after the birth of my second child! So how then, could my abs be split apart and not healed completely since pregnancy?

My heart began to race. Bladder prolapse and a split in my ab muscles could not be the correct assessments of my symptoms. And yet, even as I said that loudly in my head, I had this gouging, twisting feeling in my gut that I had crossed over to "that side of life." Was this an aging thing? Hadn't I suffered enough "down there"?

It suddenly weighed so heavily on me that all those years working through my root and sacral chakras now seemed as though the issues were never going to clear up.

"The moment you hit rock bottom and realize you have lost yourself is the exact moment you actually begin to find yourself."
~Sholina Jivraj

Every experience is an opportunity to heal something. For me, the healing of my womb, my Sacred Feminine, had to take place on all levels and over a long period of time. I have healed lifetimes of pain and trauma. Being molested as a child, emotionally and sexually abused by a narcissist, the wife of an adulterer, raped, having experienced severe trauma from the birth of my first child, surviving an excruciating, merciless divorce followed by financial loss, being completely abandoned by my family and friends, and struggling to survive as a single mom... I can't always say this with full conviction, depending on where I am in my journey, but I am a *f*cking warrior*. That's what I do. Even in my darkest days when I didn't even want to be on this earth, somehow (truthfully, I don't even know how to this day), I found the strength to keep going. Slowly but surely it does happen. I can't explain it, but I seem to have infinite assistance from the other side. Call them Angels, guides, my Divine, or whatever. If I'm ever in a situation in which I am unable to help myself and feel completely alone, some kind of force helps me rise. Every single time. I am the (s)hero of my own life. And more often than not, I am better than I was before, transforming my pain into strength, courage, and resilience.

This diagnosis was a devastating blow and I had all sorts of emotions fly around for days after. I went from feeling sorry for myself, to confusion, anger, determination, and then dejection. And then I pressed the repeat button. It was bad enough that my confidence as a woman was completely shaken, but now as a Fitness Trainer? I had so many challenges in life that threatened various aspects of me, but at least I had my body and my expertise– until now. It was just too much to swallow and I felt the Universe had crossed the line. Having a Spiritual Psychotherapy and Reiki background I understood very well that emotions, if not dealt with, manifest into physical issues. I spent years working on myself and healing the past– all that time, energy, and money. This latest issue with my pelvic floor just seemed so unfair!

"From bitter to better, from victim to victor,
from worrier to warrior."
~Sholina Jivraj

As I debated my life events in my head, I did go through the victim stage. But with time and grace, I reached the point where I could ask what the bigger purpose in all of this was. Why was there still more to all of these root and sacral issues? It wasn't long before Spirit told me that it's because I am to help other women heal the same issues– on all levels: mental, spiritual, physical, and emotional. This wasn't a new message. I had known for years that my work with women would be transformational but for the longest time I thought it involved women who were in transition; those who were ready to separate from their abusive partners. Believe me, the amount of strength, courage, and resilience it took to leave my ex, and my entire community, was enough experience to change and enrich the lives of many women in similar situations. But the Universe had bigger plans that I could not yet see.

"In order to soar, you first have to jump."
~Steve Harvey

In one moment of meditation I heard this message: when you're done, you've just begun. Sometimes, the moment when you finally reach the point where you are done with the drama and trauma, is the moment you step into the awakening that your experiences are smaller than you. I am not my experiences,. I am someone who shares their gifts with others. Clearly the Universe was encouraging me to dig so deeply that I would be in a position to help women heal their Divine Feminine; even emotional issues that have manifested into physical form. What a profound realization. I'm not gonna lie; I was getting pretty annoyed with the Universe dumping all of this on me. God knows I was ready to help on the emotional levels, but to have to experience and learn about the physical aspects of both pain and pleasure in sexuality meant more training, more feeling, more time, and more money. After all these years, I still hadn't reached the fullest expression of my life purpose. The process was daunting. It took some time and contemplation but eventually I reached a point of resolve where I could say, "Ok, I hear you, and I'll be patient enough to trust in the process. Let me be of service to others in a way that serves the highest good of all." It was time to jump.

When you are in the fitness industry, everyone around you is obsessed with how they look. They may not all admit it, and this preoccupation may look different from person to person, but it's definitely there. For example, some are more into how strong they look, others more about how young they look, and then others want to be seen as dedicated gym enthusiasts— "nothing's gonna stop me, no pain no gain" crap. It wouldn't be unexpected then, to catch chitchat around the gym on topics such as diet, bums, and aging. I make it a point to avoid these fruitless dialogues as much as possible but as a Fitness Expert, you can't help but get sucked into them from time to time. I used to listen to these women talk about their 'bingo wings', 'mummy tummy', 'hot flashes', and 'peeing a little when they jumped'. They would laugh as they all shared complaints with each other. I wondered if they were trying to make themselves feel okay about it, to justify it, since it was happening to everyone else around them. More and more, I would hear them converse on all their issues and how they chalked it up to 'getting older'. Maybe it's true that misery loves company, but I didn't want to be a part of that group, and I was okay with being the lone wolf as a result. I wanted to choose a different reality. I wanted to believe that if your hormones, diet, and workout regime were taken care of, then you could maintain enough muscle mass to avoid many of the physical breakdowns that these women were incessantly talking about. I didn't want to let any one of those things happen to me... until it did.

"To know anything, first you must begin with yourself."
~Osho

Rewinding many years back, I think I irritated people as a child— my cousins, some teachers, my fellow community members— I was often the black sheep in the family because I had this never-ending need to ask 'why?' And 'why not?' Most of the time I'd get a response like, "Because I said so," or "Because that's the way we've always done it. End of story." And most of the time, if that didn't shut me down, the stern look on my dad's face (or someone else in authority) certainly did. Regardless, you could see the emotions on my face and sense my resentment when I was forced to do (or not do) something without understanding the significance behind it. This didn't go unnoticed. But it wasn't my fault I was so curious about human behavior at such an early age. To my detriment (or so I used to think) I was very right-brain oriented and came from a position where my behavior would be based on how I felt, not what was necessarily logical or status quo. But this type of living was met with an immeasurable amount of resistance. I was constantly repressed and suppressed. I guess I was labeled as a difficult child while growing up and eventually I succumbed to the expectations of others. Don't get me wrong, there were many moments where I was rebellious towards my family and community. For example, when I refused to take my ex-husband's last name, or wore pants to religious ceremonies, or refused to let my in-laws dictate how I raised my child. I even cut off family members who were clearly manic and abusive, which goes against the belief that 'family is blood'. These smaller rebellious acts probably gave me the courage to exercise the biggest revolts a woman in my culture ever could. First, after my mother passed away, I silently renounced my religion. Second, I left my ex-husband; a man who was very actively involved in religion and the community, who was attractive, who seemed to be a good father, and was financially successful. But the status quo needed to be broken. It was no longer okay for me to be in situations that were sadistic, counterfeit, or that made me powerless. As urgent and necessary as they were, these decisions were met with serious consequences, some of which are still painful today.

As a result, I shut down some of my right-brain processes. After I left my ex, my entire world collapsed. I went from a place where all my financial needs were met and being 'taken care of' by a man who had assumed the paternal role of my father since I was barely the age of twenty. The level of dominance and control was firmly established when I begged my parents to cancel the wedding two days prior; the day I was having the sacred bridal ceremony with my family. But for more than one reason, my parents could not back out at that time. And me, being so young and immature, foolishly handed over my power in a way that would fill my life with years of regret. And so began my journey with a narcissist. I know now that he having all the control was his way of keeping me in a positon of weakness— a positon that stemmed from my childhood to adolescence. No wonder I was hit with a ton of bricks when I finally escaped him. He made sure I lost my friends and family, he corrupted my reputation in the community, and he dragged out the entire process which not only led to a significant financial loss, but slowly stripped me of my mental health. My doctor had strongly recommended that I take anti-depressants but I refused. It was such a debilitating process that I completely lost my sense of self, my self-respect, my will to live. I shut off my spiritual side for a long while and my physical body was degraded with the stress. I ended up in other abusive relationships that brought me further down into disgrace. I thought for sure there was no way out of this. There was not a chance in hell that I could ever recover from this. These days were even darker than those when my ex would sexually abuse me. If ever I thought a life experience would kill me, this was it. But somehow over the years a great shift happened. This may have been that point where I was absolutely furious with the Universe and I demanded that something change *immediately*. I was so f*cking done with life as it was and I commanded the Universe to *fix this or I was out*! I was dead serious. I stipulated that change would have to come by my next birthday, or else...

"Resilience is brilliance."
~Sholina Jivraj

Part of the shift was moving from right brain to left brain living; everything from paying the bills and organizing my home to turning to science to further enhance my yoga and fitness practice. I began to do things more logically and methodically. I stopped offering Reiki, hypnosis, and Body Psychotherapy to my clients, and even halted teaching about spirituality. My meditation practice dwindled. It seems so unusual; in times of tribulation people usually turn to God. That's how they find balance and means to cope with their dramas. I happened to go the opposite way. But today, I see this as the Universe giving me the opportunity to find my balance of yin and yang, my three dimensional world versus the spiritual. Since I always lived right-brain dominant I didn't realize it is not the most functional way to live on earth. But as lonely and difficult as that lesson was I see now that it was given to me out of grace.

"The only people who get mad at you for speaking the truth are those who are still living the lie."
~Sholina Jivraj

Have you seen that movie "How to Lose a Guy in 10 Days"? I remember in one of the final scenes when Ben Berry calls Anne Anderson out on her crap. "*Bullll shit.*" He was so matter-of-fact, and cool as a cucumber. I had to rewind and watch that part a

113

couple of times (I think that's when he finally won me over, long hair and all). As I watched that scene, it was exactly then that I realized this: I secretly love calling people out on their shit (as long as it's a topic that interests me). And there's nothing wrong with that because my intention is not to just call them out, but really to get to the truth of things. Why was I always shamed for trying to find meaning and purpose in everything? Maybe it was the delivery of my message (I'm a Sagittarius and I know we often have 'foot in mouth' disease). Or maybe people in general find it annoying when others go against the grain and disrupt the group dynamics. I don't know. Regardless, it never ceases to surprise me how society is bamboozled into accepting what is 'normal'. And although there are a million examples I could give you, the one that is relevant here is the concept of aging. There is a consciousness about getting older that has been ingrained in us because of main stream media. What we should look like, what we should wear (and at what age), what is an acceptable age difference between you and your partner, what activities we should be doing, what physical symptoms you should be experiencing as you go through hormonal changes, and of course, what medical device or drug you should take to 'fix' it all. We are bombarded with these messages in media, government, big pharma, religion, culture, communities— everywhere we turn all our senses are blasted with negative labels and images. One thing I have learned by watching other people is that when they are told a lie over and over again, eventually they will start believing it. The fact of the matter is we have no bloody clue what 'normal' is! The only thing we have to use as a basis for comparison is what we have learned from everyone else. The truth is, I won't know what my normal is until I fully learn about the way I want to live and then consciously live it in the next two decades (which will likely be against the grain). I feel it is this consciousness that elevates humanity— intellectually, spiritually, and physically.

"Honor your inner wisdom and allow yourself to heal."
~Sholina Jivraj

Back at the gym, while these women were complaining about these physical ailments, I had this nagging feeling that something wasn't right. These can't be 'natural' things that happen if you take care of your body. Yes, there are 'normal' things that happen to people all the time, but it doesn't mean it's all natural. All we are told about the typical progression of aging comes from sources that only benefit from our degrading bodies. When we all follow the common protocols of diet, fitness, and health care, we fall into a typical pattern which is perceived as 'normal'– for example, losing flexibility or having poor digestion as you get older. Yet, I have seen people with my own eyes live strong and healthy lives way past 100. These are people who live differently than most North Americans in that they have a movement practice every day, they don't heed to the hustle and bustle of life, and they live simply. By the same token, I have also seen people who follow the nutrition, supplement, and vaccine guidelines given to us by healthcare and government institutions and still get cancer, heart disease, shingles, and Alzheimer's. No. All these 'normal' ailments just didn't make sense to me.

In my own quest for answers, I searched extensively for information from experts in the field of natural medicine and nutrition. I have found enough material to believe that what we are taught is normal can very well be a lie. I believe that if we didn't follow the typical North American diet and remove unnecessary stressors we could have a completely different life. I believe that the nutrients from fresh, live foods and lots of water will nourish our bodies and help in cell regeneration and anti-aging. I believe that we can feel younger if we just make time to move, play, and be creative. Imagine if we breathed fresh air by spending a few minutes in nature every day. How would it look if we spent more time engaging in our communities rather than watching fake news? What if we felt so good about ourselves, knowing we were enough, that we stopped chasing the dreams of mass consumerism? We would never need to search outside of ourselves to feel joy and passion because it would already exist within us. As a result, I intuitively feel that there would be less of a need for addictions such as sugar, technology, drugs and alcohol.

*"If you don't make courageous choices for yourself,
nobody else will."*
~James Altucher

Ladies, I can't say this loud enough: it's time to take your power back! It saddens me that so many women easily succumb to accepting what the world dictates what their reality should be. It grieves me that we just accept what someone in a higher position of power tells us is our truth around health, religion, and materialism. Maybe reflecting on the next several questions can lead you to a more empowered path: Who do you think has your best interests at heart when it comes to your health? Are we that disempowered that we don't question what is really happening? Do we not have the courage to find alternative ways to heal our bodies rather than our current healthcare options? What if you had all the utmost support through your pregnancy and delivery– enough rest, someone to assist with natural child birth to avoid tears or using forceps, and wearing the right support for your abdomen to allow the body to heal itself? And what if you could take as much time off as you needed without repercussions or feeling guilty that someone was helping with the baby? What if you had stronger boundaries around sex? What if you stopped saying 'yes' to people when you really meant 'no'? What if you could heal all the abuse you endured as a woman and freed yourself through forgiveness? What if you refused to be a victim of your past? What if you found a man who made you feel safe, loved, and supported and never, ever have to feel like you are in a situation because you have no choice? Who would you be? How would you feel? It's time to change our world and let the Divine Feminine emerge with conviction. It's time to break free from the old patterns of thought, expectations, and the submission that continue to disempower us. When I finally reached this place, I was determined to make a difference. It sparked a burning desire to educate and inspire women for change.

However despite all of these strong and honorable convictions, there was still the problem of having to stop for pee breaks on long car rides, going to pee before I taught my class 'just in case,' waking up at night to pee, low back pain, and this annoying, 'mummy tummy' that was starting to creep up on me. It was exasperating! Looking back, even before the frequent pit stops began, for about a year I felt pre sure, sometimes pain in the lower abdominal area, and I noticed that using tampons felt 'different'. To be honest, it wasn't even these symptoms that made me go to the Pelvic Floor Physiotherapist. It was actually because my sex life was definitely changing in that I went from a multiple orgasms to just a few, eventually down to one or none. (Yes, you read that right.) I know there are various reasons why women have trouble achieving orgasm. But in this instance, I knew it was due to the prolapse of my bladder. My 'vajayjay' was at the onset of depression and so was I. I lived in a sexless marriage for so many years; even when we did have sex it was pretty bad and often left me loathing myself, especially when it was forced upon me. Imagine after that to have finally broken free from that prison and found a partner who shared my desires, had a high drive, and was really good at making me feel pleasure, I needed things to work properly down there! Imagine how embarrassing this was! I really felt less of a woman. I was afraid that my boyfriend at the time would think I was getting older. There was already an age difference between us and this would only make me more insecure about that. We had a very active sex life from the beginning, but because it was becoming more and more uncomfortable for me, we had to practice a little abstinence. And although he was anxious to get this problem fixed (we both were!) he was so loving and supportive. He encouraged me to keep searching for answers.

It was not enough to have the diagnosis and to correct the problem. I had to question why these things happened, what it was that I needed to do to fix it or prevent it from getting worse, and to share the insights with other women who had fallen into the 'this is how it is' trap. The more I asked why and how, the more I was shocked to find out that there were so many contributing factors to what we were likely experiencing. I couldn't believe it! There really isn't enough education to help women understand the consequences of some of their actions and experiences that are slowly debilitating their bodies. We have been lied to; lies about the knowledge and 'expertise' of the medical community being superior to that of the sisterhood, lies about the best fitness and health practices, lies about proper nutrition. The real truth is the effects of certain exercises, difficult pregnancies or labor, bad posture, and poor breathing habits are disastrous to the pelvic floor. Unfortunately, we simply accept that 'physical degradation comes with aging' because we are in an endless state of disem-powerment allowing other people and institutions to dictate our experiences while big pharma continues to reap the benefits of the cash grab. In my gut, I strongly believe this to be true.

No. I had lived too many years in sadness, pain, and frustration. I could not simply accept what was happening. I needed a good– no, a *great* life; one where I could still enjoy my body, the deliciousness of sex, and be blissfully in love with a partner who I was crazy passionate about. Besides, it was in my nature to ask why! It probably got me into more trouble than anything growing up, but it's what makes me such a strong teacher and healer today. I learn, I heal, I teach. I learn why and not just how, I walk the damn talk, and then I teach my clients the same. Knowledge is power. Literally! I especially see this with my clients in my signature Yoga-Flex-Fit™ classes. They are more empowered and motivated because of the very fact that when they know *why* they are doing a physical exercise (or why not), *why* they need more mobility exercises, or *why* they need to learn to breathe all over again, they are more invested in their wellness and self-care. When they are more invested, they take these skills outside the class and apply them to their everyday world. They continue to reinforce the good habits they learned so they have the power to enhance their lives every single day. They can heal their back and neck pain just by being more aware of their everyday movements. Unlike a typical yoga class in which you are Zen for about an hour, I can educate you and help you to improve the most critical component to better health– your posture– which (with practice) will last for years to come. Every hip rotation or extension, every thoracic breath, every anterior or posterior tilt of the pelvis has significant consequences not only to the corrective exercise at hand but also to your body's alignment in everything you do. Once this is understood you can take these essential skills and apply them to everyday activities (like standing, lying down, getting in and out of bed, squatting, or bending over) to prevent misalignment and pain. How *empowering* is this knowledge?

The fact of the matter is, if you want to change your physique, prevent health issues, and maximize your strength, you have to understand how and why your body works. Furthermore, just because one thing works for one person, doesn't mean the same will work for another. And this may be difficult for some yoga enthusiasts to hear, but just because there is an ancient tradition that worked for people in the past, doesn't mean the same exact practice will work for people in the present. We are not the same bodies as the ancients who practiced all sorts of movement throughout the day - they worked the fields, they danced and played barefoot. We, on the other hand, are over-stressed and bombarded with environmental toxins. But the single most vicious habit is that we sit for eight, twelve, fourteen hours a day. As a result, we have terrible posture and weak gluts; and this creates a snowball of negative effects. Poor posture tightens your shoulders, neck, chest, and core muscles. Once there is limited movement in these areas with each breath the intra-abdominal pressure increases, causing compression on the pelvic floor. Excess pressure then weakens the pelvic floor and core muscles, resulting in back and pelvic pain, as well as sexual dysfunctions. We then go to yoga to build strength and flexibility, and are told over and over again to take a belly breath, all the while not able to stabilize the pressure anywhere else which exacerbates those same issues! Then to further aggravate our back issues, we do backbends without taking proper precautions of stabilizing the glutes or the shoulder girdle. *And you wonder why so many people have issues after doing yoga?*

Combining fitness, yoga, and body mechanics is the key to a remarkable movement practice that is functional and promotes wellness for every body. At the time of my pelvic health journey, this was my philosophy in fitness and yoga. So when I started studying more about pelvic floor health, why would my approach be any different?

"Hindsight is 20/20, unless you are an intuitive."
~Sholina Jivraj

It feels a bit ridiculous to me, with how this information all comes together, that I didn't figure it out sooner myself. I knew and felt that there was something missing, that something big was coming my way but I had no idea what that was. It's hard to explain, but I felt as though everything I learned (and was still learning) had a bigger purpose. I believe that all experiences have a deeper meaning; so there had to be more to this than just sharing with other women to help with or prevent the same challenges. I felt that there was something even more powerful that was to be discovered; something about sacred sexuality that would bring a certain vitality and dynamism to the lives of women that was long overdue and totally overlooked. Ladies, if you are reading up to this point, it is likely that you can either identify with some of the things I'm sharing, or you are an empowered, out of the box thinker, or you intuitively know that there is something *powerful* in this information I am sharing with you. Either way, I want to say thank you for letting me share my story.

"There is both pain and power in persistence."
~Sholina Jivraj

After the stage two pelvic floor organ prolapse and diastasis recti diagnoses, of course undergoing Pelvic Floor Physiotherapy alone was not enough for me because I needed to cover every single base to fix my problem. And so I went back to my training materials on fixing organ prolapse and diastasis recti– a very specific breathing apnea course I had taken about a year-and-a-half back. Funny that I never took it very seriously because I never, in a million years, thought I would have to deal with this dysfunction. Isn't it interesting though, how the Universe set me up for that training just before the sh*t hit the fan? I immediately researched more on this topic and found out that (on top of poor choice of exercises), pregnancy, difficult child birth, imbalanced hormones, and sexual trauma all had a critical impact on pelvic floor function. Unfortunately, I had all of those too. It's almost as if there were no contributing factors that I didn't have; and the more I researched, the more the walls were closing in on me. (Really Universe? I guess a good teacher is an experienced one- literally. Leave no stone unturned. Lucky me.) I felt resentful and angry but continued to educate myself because rolling over and giving up my sex life was *not* an option. And even though I already knew the answer to the question I kept asking myself: How could this be happening? I seriously started to stress about the health of my vajayjay. My pants were not fitting me anymore because my lower belly was protruding from the prolapse. I felt pressure even as I sat and did nothing. I had to stop many exercises that I was so used to doing, I had to fit in time to do my relaxation exercises every day. My entire routine had changed! My classes were no longer 'hard-core'. I had to stop all cardio exercises which reduced the amount of dopamine (feel good hormones) in my body, and my self-confidence nose-dived. My purpose and passion was to help others; yet I knew that I couldn't help anyone when I looked in the mirror and hated what I saw. I was now feeling depressed. *I did not come this far in my life to live it moderately!* I needed answers, fast!

I decided to discuss the training technique with the physiotherapist. But, because she (and most pelvic floor physiotherapists) didn't understand what it was at first, she was not okay with me doing it in case it worsened my condition. I, like many women, had a hyper-tonic pelvic floor. It was too tight. (All those ab crunches, planks, and Kegel exercises only exacerbated my condition without me being the wiser. In fact, I learned there were so many other 'exercises' I taught in fitness class that were detrimental to women's health; I just didn't realize it at the time). Since the therapist didn't want me to practice the technique, and since I'm not okay with being told not to do something for no real reason, I did the breathing technique right in front of her (literally while she was checking inside my vagina) to show her that the practice didn't further tighten my pelvic floor. And of course, she was amazed at the effect of everything being pulled upwards in its rightful place. I explained that the method I used strengthened the muscles *eccentrically* (in their longer position) and not *concentrically* (in the shorter, tighter position) so it was completely safe and effective. Since then, she has sent me clients who suffer from prolapse! So while she helped me relax and strengthen my pelvic floor muscles using her methods, I worked on lifting everything upwards and re-integrating my core, including *fixing the diastasis recti.* Finally, some hope of improvement on the physical side of things; but emotionally there was a continuous mishmash of relief, hope, self-pity, determination, and fear. I had to hang onto hope in order to find the moments in which I was excited to get my life back on track.

Unfortunately, only a couple of weeks into the breathing technique, I found that when I did it I felt pain in my stomach that didn't ease up. And it didn't take long to understand that the pain was inflammation due to "leaky gut". So, as much as my vajayjay wanted me to focus on the pelvic floor rehab, I needed to heal my gut first. Frustrated and powerless it seemed like this was never going to go away. For me, healing my gut was a very long and frustrating process because there was continuous damage for such a long period of time. It's true, patience is not my virtue, but I needed to speed up the healing of my gut so I could go back to enjoying my libido (which was getting near *extinct* with all this commotion)– talk about a great motivating factor! ""leaky gut"" was not a new ailment to me. I had digestive issues from way back in 2008. Years of bloat that progressed into chronic conditions had (now I know) destroyed my deeper core muscles (even though I still had a six pack!). But the doctor only wanted to give me something to treat the symptoms, which I had to use from time to time because of the pain. For a long while, I couldn't eat anywhere but home, and eventually was down to one shake a day. Eventually, my doctor referred me to a gastroenterologist. But I didn't go. Because I didn't take the medicine on a regular basis or go for the gastroscopy procedure with the specialist, my doctor was getting annoyed that I kept coming back for the same issue. What could I do? I didn't want to take the meds (and I was too chicken to go for the scope). I needed to heal the gut lining and I knew the drugs were really not helping with the root of the problem; if anything they were probably hard on my liver. I continued to research and realized I had to remove all inflammatory foods from my diet– foods that were supposed to be a part of a normal, healthy diet; all wheat, dairy, corn, and sugar had to be eliminated.

When you are questioning things, you have to know that you won't always like the answers you get. But I'll tell you that if you turn a blind eye to some things just because it goes against the way you were taught by your parents, teachers, doctors, or other influential figures, *you are choosing to continue to disempower yourself.* Just follow where the money is and you will find truth. Whoever is making the most amount of money or has the most power in the world is (without a doubt) the same people or institutions that are controlling the information you receive about you and your health. When we don't question, we can get sick. Issues can become chronic. It's needless suffering for you and your families. All the while, big pharma continues to cash out.

I continued to suffer for months (which grew into years) and used over the counter medications to address the same symptoms without treating the cause. I saw a naturopath, an acupuncturist, a spiritual healer, I got colonics, and took supplements. I even reached out to Shamans for plant medicines. I spent thousands of dollars on my gut. The process required a lot of time and energy that I didn't have. I felt sick and unmotivated all the time. But, in all honesty, I learned from every single wellness professional I worked with. I learned about adrenals, cortisol, thyroid, and how the balance of hormones is absolutely crucial to good health. The problem if you are stressed, especially chronic stress is that you will never resolve the other issues. Stress is the killer of many—not always quick and agile, but a powerful force that sucks the joy right out of life and eventually leads to a slow and painful death. In North America, it is normal for people to be in a continuous state of stress, but it sure isn't natural. In our natural state, there is no self-induced negative stress. It is the major culprit that causes inflammation, and inflammation is the major player in the onset of disease. Once you have inflammation in the gut, all your hormones are completely thrown off; it becomes a snowball effect. Disease can slowly creep up on you because by the time you know that you have adrenal fatigue and thyroid issues (due to stress) your hormones have been off for so long that treatment becomes much more complex, and it becomes timely and chaotic. Unfortunately, I was subjected to chronic stress for so long in my marriage, and through the subsequent separation and divorce. Being married to a narcissist is one thing; trying to divorce one is another. Unless you (or someone close to you) have been through it, you have no idea of the devastating effects of their mind control and gas-lighting capabilities. Multiply this over the years and through an ugly, incapacitating divorce with no support system (he literally sabotaged my relationship with friends and family, save for the three closest people to me), I hit rock bottom. On all levels: mind, body, emotion, and spirit. I was a complete mess. It would be easy for me to say that if had I known the snowball effects of stress earlier,I would have looked after myself while I was living through the divorce. But when you are actually living in the incessant wrath of a narcissist and his sociopathic behavior, you are in constant survival mode. Period. You can't focus for long on anything else. But sometimes, in order to shut a door, you have to first step into darkness.

Thankfully all the knowledge that I had gained helped me to achieve the right mindset this time. Since I had found a wonderful homeopathic doctor who also practiced osteopathy and used Biofeedback Therapy, I knew there was an excellent possibility that I could beat "leaky gut" for good. She was addressing all of my issues at the same time. I covered all my bases for physical, mental, emotional, and spiritual healing. It was a commitment- financially, physically, and mentally for sure, but with high hope of healing this on all levels and getting back to pleasure in the bedroom, I was committed! So I remained steadfast on the dietary changes for "leaky gut". I had already cut out most dairy many years earlier when my second daughter was born intolerant to cow's milk. Back then, I learned about the history of dairy farmers and the toxicity of milk due to high levels of antibiotics given to the cows. I committed to removing foods that were harder to digest (like nuts, raw food, all grains, and caffeine) and adding tons of healing foods (like squash, kefir, and healthy fats). I also added lots of water to my diet. All my meals were prepared at home. I eventually started seeing improvements; not just less bloat and fewer mood swings, but better sleep and energy levels. However, I still had months of treatment before I could continue pelvic floor rehab.

"If you want to glow, let sh*t go."
~Sholina Jivraj

If all of this wasn't enough, the icing on the cake was when the smug little women in my class would comment on my weight gain. (Apparently this doesn't just happen in high school, and it sure did bring back some painful memories. How many times have we been in the line of fire from a jealous, insecure girl or woman?) But knowing that misery loves company, I refused to roll over and play the 'age' card with them. They could be the catty little women that they were and it didn't have to affect me. After all, they learned this behavior as 'normal' for women to be competitive in our society, but let me say it's not 'natural'. Women used to be a sisterhood who supported each other through all things in life (including nursing another woman back to health after childbirth, which very likely prevented pelvic floor dysfunction, I might add). They understood that to survive and thrive we needed to work together and bring each other up rather than pull each other down. That being said, as part of this entire process I had to evaluate and feel, very deeply, my emotions around being a woman. I had to address some of my false beliefs and take my power back in certain situations in order to alleviate the physical discomfort. I had to forgive tons. Me. Others. Me again. It's an ongoing process of course, because there are so many layers to healing. But as a result, I have allowed and empowered myself to relieve much of the 'pressure' I felt in my pelvic area for years– pressures of being a woman, wife, and mother, as well as the pressures I felt from my sexual partners. I used Emotional Freedom Technique (EFT), a trauma release exercise, and free-style movement to transform the darkness. All of this work was emotionally taxing, but not in a negative way. Realizing and feeling the heaviness of so much stuff I was hanging onto, feeling the burden of it all - that was the work. I had to let that sh*t go. Even though I could feel that I was on the verge of a breakthrough, I longed for the time when this could all be resolved and I could find peace again. I continued to ask for spiritual help and, as always, my prayers were answered with grace, although not in the timelines that my ego would have wanted. But I realize now that the fruition of something new and beautiful is directly in proportion to your willingness to let go of the old.

Throughout the process I did more research. I continued my education in body mechanics and began to understand the relationship between poor posture and pelvic floor health. I learned some surprising things. You know when you see women in magazines – dancers, or actresses who stick their ass out more than they are supposed to? We label that as sexy. Well, that continued anterior tilt of the pelvis overstretches the abdominals and tightens up the lower back, inhibiting the proper function of your core, eventually causing pain and discomfort. I also learned that some crunchless ab exercises were contributing factors to worsening Diastasis Recti. Squats and lunges can also be detrimental to poor pelvic floor health. I eliminated the infamous belly breath and learned to breathe in a way that stabilized the intra-abdominal pressure. I eliminated Kegels– an absolutely destructive tool if one has a hypertonic (tight) vajayjay. You have to absolutely use these exercises in moderation and only when your pelvic floor is relaxed, a process that also takes time and training. Full planks, reverse curls, poor posture, sitting all day, Kegels– all of these were killing me and all of these were learned from fitness professionals or doctors– all because I took their word at face value!

The more I questioned and researched all of these things: "leaky gut", candida, and pelvic floor, the more I realized that there was indeed a snowball effect. Pregnancy and sexual or birth trauma compromises the pelvic floor. Chronic bloat and anterior tilt of the pelvis massacres the transverse ab muscles (the muscles that 'corset' the abs). Ignorant choices in core exercises create an imbalance in the entire core. Poor posture and breath affects intra-abdominal pressure. And all of these conditions create weak pelvic floor, low back pain, and organ prolapse. Why didn't I put two and two together before? It sounds so simple now. If any part of your core muscles are compromised or dysfunctional, obviously it will affect the all the others. It's not rocket science! But it is something that was simply over-looked because of incorrect training, and treating issues as though they were individual and separate from the whole. I was finally coming to a breakthrough!

"Reclaiming your passion for yourself makes you irresistible to others."
~Sholina Jivraj

The last mile. Thank goodness for this beautiful soul, who is a holistic nutritionist, I met on my journey. She educated me about a miracle supplement of just fruits and veggies. If I'm truly honest, I tried the product out of desperation because I was still impatient about the healing process and just needed that final thing to get me to the tipping point. I was sure it was a miracle that in just a few weeks' time I got rid of the remaining bloat! I was shocked and thrilled at the same time. On top of that I had better skin, more energy, no joint pain, and I even managed to change my PH level to a more neutral state– I had been trying to do that for years! Most significantly, with the elimination of inflammation, I was finally able to do the breathing apneas without any pain! I didn't go back to the pelvic floor physiotherapist because I knew this modality would work. It took some time and diligence to relax and strengthen my pelvic floor, but I am so, so happy to tell you that my vajayjay is back in business. I don't know how I survived for all those months without my multiple O's (which by the way, are stronger than ever), but I do know that I will never be in that situation again. Sexual health is a very important component to joy, happiness, and creativity– at least it is for me. And as part of rebuilding that component, I learned about tantras and sacred sexuality. I learned to use the power of orgasm to heal sexual trauma, to sky-rocket my artistic vision, and rediscovered sensuality. It was a turn back to right-brain thinking, or more specifically, heart-centered living. It is no coincidence that life has turned in such a way that I have attracted new and beautiful relationships with like-minded people. I have allowed more love into my life. I go to bed early and wake up early. I've begun my meditation practice again. I spend time in nature, and am more productive than ever. I'm taking better care of my health by eating raw, live foods. My home is more organized and there's a general feeling of joy and peace around us. It's as though I have finally found a comfortable balance between right and left-brain living. It's a totally new experience for me!

"A belief is just a thought you keep thinking."
~Abraham Hicks

It hasn't been easy to get here. You can't get here if you are not ready to face the emotional and spiritual aspects of poor pelvic floor health. You have to dig deep and address the darker emotions and beliefs you may have internalized all the way from sexual trauma down to less severe experiences that may have once seemed insignificant to you. This can include having sex when you didn't want to, with a partner you didn't want to have sex with, having a partner who enters you too quickly or who is selfish in their sexuality. Emotional residue can also manifest physically if you ever felt trapped in an abusive relationship, have been ashamed of your past relationships, ashamed of your body, been put down because of your emotional sensitivity during PMS, or not honoring your own sexual needs. You have learned these behaviors because of false belief systems. Maybe you believe that as a woman you have to sacrifice everything you have. Maybe you believe that men are more powerful than women. Or maybe you believe that you are a victim of your circumstances. These are false beliefs.

Unfortunately, we have lived too long in a world where the Divine Feminine is not honored. Our sacred feminine sexuality has been buried for so many years that it almost seems normal to live in the way of the masculine and disqualifying the immeasurable gifts of the feminine. But, if you look, listen, and feel what is happening around the world today, we are at the brink of a feminine uprising. Perhaps you have noticed that structures of the old ways are starting to collapse. There are big changes in politics, religion, and business as they do not have the same dominance they once had. This is the time of break*down* which is necessary until we reach the break*through*. Watch and you will see the rise of spirituality, compassion, and oneness. The energy is all around us. There is something within you that is always longing for something more, something that does not like the false boundaries and restrictions that have been put upon you in a masculine world. Whatever you may be right now, whoever you may be right now, you want to be something *more* and you have an inner knowing that it is possible.

This calling is from the Divine Feminine. It's up to you to answer her call.

"No matter how hard it tries, a ripple that laps onto the ocean shore will never be as powerful as the ocean that created it. The goal is to be the ocean– the central force in our existence that moves mountains, creates all life, shakes continents, and is respected by everyone."
~James Altucher

Have you ever taken a look back at events in your life and finally realize that as painful as they were, they were worth it? You realize how strong you really are, that you are meant to heal, and that you can take the gifts from the experiences and share them with others. It seems like my entire life was setting me up for what I know and do today. It is my dream to teach, heal, and empower others. I didn't gain all my expertise from books. I learned from experience and because I continuously asked for answers. I cannot afford to take a passive approach to healing. My inner warrior has big dreams and high hopes of what I want this life to be, and there is simply no room for me to roll over and accept what is 'normal'.

Reclaim your magnificence, my sisters, because no one else is going to do it for you. Remember that no one can love you more than you can love yourself, and everyone will treat you the way you treat yourself. Those rose colored glasses will not help you if your head is buried in the sand. *Knowledge is your power.* Only today can I say this with utter conviction. So be powerful, ladies! Say 'no' when you need to. Ask 'why?' And 'why not?' Don't stop until you understand enough to make the right decisions for you. After all, *this is your life.* Yes, it can be painful when truth brings darkness to light. But time heals most wounds. It's true. The journey to the mountain top can be frustrating, lonely, and even exhausting. But you must keep climbing. Let your Divine Feminine guide you and give you the strength to powerfully climb higher so that you are able to pick up all the gifts that await you: sacred sex, pleasure, sensuality, loving relationships, creativity, peace, grace, and beauty.

I'll meet you at the top, my friend. And be prepared to be astounded because it's a totally different view from up here.

Sholina Jivraj is a Fitness, Yoga, Posture, and Pelvic Floor Specialist. With a thirst for knowledge and a passion for teaching, Sholina's work is both, unique and transformational in that it is the alchemy of functional movement patterns taken from fitness and yoga, the science of body mechanics, and psycho-spiritual or environmental causes of disease in the body. Her additional training as Reiki Master, Spiritual Counselor, Hypnotist, Past-Life Regressionist, and Angel Card Reader brings the East to the West for an integrative approach to fitness, moving people move from pain to power.

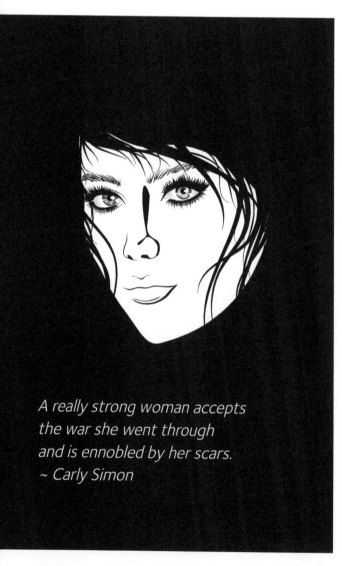

A really strong woman accepts the war she went through and is ennobled by her scars.
~ Carly Simon

Maimah Karmo

The Fearless Warrior

Every version of our selves demands a new version of our selves; much like a rebirth.

It is similar to our actual spiritual selves being birthed into human form – the painful pushing, kicking, screaming, and arching of our souls into a brand new world. Since, as human beings, we are afraid of change, transformation comes to us through circumstances we wouldn't call to ourselves. Transformation is often unwanted, because it requires the shedding of our identities, it requires us to question our existence and it shakes up our lives. But, in order for us to grow, we must learn to embrace change, for it is a gift.

My story began in Liberia, West Africa. One of the earliest memories I have is of me standing and looking out the window at the rain. In Liberia it rained in sheets, and when it did, the dry earth was drenched and hungrily soaked up the drops of water. Physically, I felt as if I was alone, yet, I knew spiritually that I was not. I was surrounded by angels. A part of me knew that I was in the world, but not of it. I had an otherworldly knowingness that I was birthed into this human child body, but was not of it, and in that place I lived, but never felt that I belonged.

When I was eight years old I had a dream. In my dream I was having a conversation with God; and he told me that my life would have challenges, but no matter what, He would always be with me. I knew then, that my life would never be ordinary. I awakened from that dream a silent warrior. I knew that whatever happened in life,

I would be someone who changed others' lives, minds, hearts, and directed others to the paths of their souls. I would be a quiet catalyst.

Within months of having that dream, Liberia broke out in war. The year was 1980. My family fled then, and returned after the war. We fled two more times. The third time, we never returned, as all of our belongings were stolen, ravaged and destroyed.

At a young age, I learned the meaning of life, sacrifice, conversation with God, heart and soul over material things and I knew that my human body was just the shell that housed the mission, ministry and mastery of soul purpose that was before me. I didn't know what to expect, but I knew that God would lead my way. I saw myself as a fearless warrior, with a crown of hearts, a heart laced with courage, my hips girded by faith and strength, my feet wrapped in discernment, my body cloaked with protection, and wielding my sword of love. This image of myself would serve me well, over and over again. I had no idea what was yet to come.

On February 28, 2006, at 4:45pm, I was diagnosed with Stage 2 breast cancer. The trajectory of my life changed. The next eleven years was spent working to create change in the lives of others— being a catalyst and a warrior. Besides the birth of my daughter, no other experience had transformed my life in such a powerful way— one experience was the birthing of life through me— God breathing into a new creation that manifested through my body. The other experience was looking death in the face and having everything I knew of my life, all at once fall apart, yet become crystal clear.

After being diagnosed with breast cancer, I thought that my transformation was complete. However, it was only the beginning. The Universe calls upon us over and over to evolve. I was taking baby steps, but situations continued to pop up that would nearly break me. Life would push me over and over again to pull myself up off the floor and dig into myself, calling out that inner warrior to get me through.

In 2013, I got an email from a friend's sister. Michael had committed suicide. He had hung himself. I fell to the floor. He had been one of the most brilliant, wonderful people I had ever met. He mentored kids, he helped others, he was kind and he was funny as all get out. Yet, he lived with depression, and his inner voice would constantly judge, criticize, eviscerate, and create situations that were not there, spinning him into a downward cycle, that left him hanging from a rope in his apartment. Again, I found myself broken into pieces. The hurt was too much. I loved Michael so deeply. My heart was shattered. I couldn't stop crying. I was inconsolable. I assumed personal responsibility— even though none of it was my fault, but I wondered what I could have done, by showing up more, by pushing myself to be braver in my soul work that may have possibly helped him. Months passed and I couldn't seem to get my life back together. I lived in a fog. The tears constantly poured out from me. A good friend recommended that I go to a retreat. On the way there I got totally lost. My car GPS wasn't working and then my phone and IPad died. I was stuck on a one-lane road in a rural area, with no idea of where to go. I pulled over, and called to God and my angels out loud, "Please help me get to where I need to go." Then I got back on the road. I would rely on my inner compass to get me through this. Out of nowhere appeared a little restaurant. I went in to charge my electronics, and then got back on the road. It turns out that the place I was going to was just around the corner.

When I finally arrived at the lodge, a lady looked at me as if startled, and quickly looked away. The next morning I would learn why. She told me that when I entered the room, there was an angel behind me. He was tall, bright and beautiful, and his name was Michael. "He guided you here," she said. Then she told me, "He wants you to know that there was nothing you could have done to save him. You loved him the best you could. He also wants me to tell you that you are loved by the greatest love of all. Share that love." She wrote the words on a heart and gave it to me. I still have it on my bathroom wall today.

So what did this all mean? It meant that I needed to no longer be afraid of showing up. If the greatest love of all lived within me, I needed to not be afraid to show up. Michael's death became another defining moment in my life. I began to be open, vulnerable and brave in a way that I never had before. You see, other people's lives depend on us showing up.

Inspired by Michael's life and transition, I knew that it was time to begin the next phase of my work. My experience with breast cancer had called me to break open in a way that I never had before, but God was calling me to do deeper light work. I knew that I was a healer, a catalyst for others, a silent warrior, and a soul worker. I knew that God wanted me on a bigger stage. I needed to stop being scared.

I began to listen more closely to God – and I had to make time to do this. He told me to create a digital magazine around 'bliss', and so I did. Next I felt propelled to launch a podcast, so I did. Then, I felt the inner nudge to create a workshop series called I Manifest Bliss, but in my mind, it was too much. You see, when I was helping breast cancer patients, I was doing that work to help others. This new 'I Manifest Bliss Experience' would call on me to be vulnerable in every way, if I wanted others to do the same and to heal. I had envisioned this type of event more than six years ago, but had to allow for the space between then and now, in order for me to evolve and mature enough spiritually, into a place where I was confident enough to show up as who I was, and allow the vision to boldly unfold. I'd envisioned an event where people came together for a day of soul work, sharing their stories in a series of powerful, authentic conversations, looking deep within, unearthing, and through this sharing, and inspiring awakenings and shifts in the attendees.

I launched the first event thinking I'd have 20 people; nearly 50 came. We ran out of room, so some people had to stand up and others stood outside the room. At the end of the event, everyone asked, "When is the next one?" I had not thought that far yet. I had the next one in September. I'd planned for 50 people, and more than 150 came. I was shocked and in awe of the magic that was happening. I was also truly realizing for the first time what I'd said many times was true, "When we live in our truth and are brave enough to show up vulnerably, others will too." The work we were doing at the I Manifest Bliss Experience was life transforming.

Recently, I had another powerful experience. This would shift my spiritual transformation into another stratosphere.

Life is truly a series of experiences that call upon us to show up as the powerful beings we are. In every experience, we are faced with the truth of ourselves, challenged with our idea of who we think we are, versus who we show up as when the pedal hits the metal and the rubber hits the road. I recently held another I Manifest Bliss Experience. This was our most powerful one yet. I was basking in the emotions of the day. During the event time stopped – and we were all wrapped in a beautiful web of powerful storytelling, transformation and deepening love for self and others. When the event wrapped up I didn't want it to end. I was eager to see how the Universe would integrate these lessons into all of our lives, and where the transformation would take us. When the elevator came we got in – ten deep – talking and laughing, basking in the energy of the day. We were going to have dinner together, and then I was going to head home to my daughter.

The elevator started to go down... I felt a bounce, then a jolt. Then, it stopped. The Universe wasn't going to wait. We were being called to integrate what we'd just learned, and to manifest the soul work we'd just started. As several people in the elevator panicked, I found myself growing eerily calm. Initially, I began using the word 'stuck', but I realized that we were not stuck at all, but that this limbo, this cocoon, being together in the elevator was a microcosm of our lives. We were confronted with the reality of ourselves, as we hung in a limbo between our past and our future. We had 45 minutes to reckon with our truths.

"What do you do when God doesn't want you to wait to grow tomorrow, but wants you to start today?"

"What do you do when you are forced to confront yourself and it's uncomfortable?"

"What do you do when you find yourself in the middle of here and there, and you are forced to become the catalyst that you seek?"

Within those 45 minutes we had to manifest all the shit that we had learned that day, and it was beautiful to see the transformation – while we hung in limbo, between our past and our future. We had to walk in the truths that we had talked about. Here are some of my observations of our elevator processing.

• One of the things I talk about is that the soul always knows what we need to evolve, and our 10 souls could not wait. We came to the event that day with the desire to accomplish rapid self transformation. Our human selves have this idea that things have to take time to happen, but that's a figment of our storytelling. We can manifest in an instant. Many thought we were in a crisis, but we weren't – we were creating something magical on a whole other level. When faced with your fears, anxieties, other personalities, panic, and the swirl of human emotions, do you manifest as the higher soul self you truly are, or do you melt into a puddle of emotion and forget who you were born to be? On an even deeper level, the experience called us to look at who we surround ourselves with. If you were to be trapped in an elevator for 45 minutes, are the people closest to you people you'd want to be 'stuck' with?

• In life, sometimes we think that we are stuck. We are never stuck. We were where we were supposed to be and we have every spiritual resource at our disposal– if we recognize them as such, our truth isn't just what we say, but the truth of our lives shows up as who we surround ourselves with. We can never be stuck in life because we have angels everywhere around us. The other truth of the matter is that we need to 'see' these angels around and recognize that the friends, family and strangers we take for granted are actually put into our lives for a reason, and we need each other. Each person gave each other something during those 45 minutes that enabled them to look at his or herself and grow. One of my favorite parts of the Bible is 1 Corinthians 12:12-27. It says, "There is one body, but it has many parts. But all its many parts make up one body... And so we are formed into one body... So the body is not made up of just one part. It has many parts. God has put together all the parts of the body. And he has given more honor to [all] parts. All of them will take care of one another. If one part suffers, every part suffers with it. If one part is honored, every part shares in its joy. You are the body of Christ. Each one of you is a part of it."

• We must train ourselves to notice our thoughts, and to be aware of where our minds are taking us. 'Stuck' as we were, hanging in mid-air, all the iterations of what could happen ran though our minds, but we had to be mindful of our thoughts. We had to make a choice - allow ourselves to panic or focus on the fact that the Universe might just be conspiring in our favor.

• We had to push from within to shift our thinking. Were we stuck or were we in a place where we had to rapidly grow? How do we view life's experiences - as victims, or do we realize that in every moment life is calling US to be catalysts for transformation? Another powerful truth is that we are the ones we have been looking for! What we need is not outside of us! It is within! We are the catalysts. We are the game-changers. We are the sparks that change the world!

• There were some amazing light and energy workers on that elevator, and we had to remember that, because we didn't know how long we were going to be in there. It can be a challenge to 'be the light' when you're scared shitless, but realizing and stepping into a place where you can be a light to guide and inspire others is powerful.

• As we are evolving, we find ourselves in situations where we could easily revert to former versions of ourselves - less spiritually mature, less centered, less sure, less connected with soul. Manifestation is about holding the highest vision of you and striving in every moment to create and live there.

The experience of being 'trapped' in the elevator forever changed our lives. No matter how 'small' we might see ourselves, we are powerful manifestors - powerful beyond measure, in every moment calling into our lives experiences that enable us to live as God's expression in human form. And so, we must continue to be brave. We must continue to be strong. We must continue to be love. And, I will continue to pursue my bliss; and I will live my life as a fearless warrior.

Maimah Karmo is living the American Dream. Born in Liberia, West Africa, she escaped 3 wars and fled to the USA at 15, alone. She is a breast cancer survivor, founder of the Tigerlily Foundation, bestselling author, podcaster and inspirational leader with her I Manifest Bliss events.
Maimah sits on Congressional panels, and she is a highly sought out Media Influencer featured on Oprah, Good Morning America, The Today Show, Cosmopolitan, Essence, and more, and contributor to Huffington Post and Forbes Magazine.
Most dear to her is Noelle, her 15-year-old daughter.

Nikki-Monique Kurnath

SingGirlMumMe

*"She thought she wanted a Knight in Shining Armor but
what she really needed was a Heroine with a Shining Sword."*
~NMK

Being a Mom is a rewarding lifetime role to be blessed with. But let's face all the facts here... it's also one of the toughest roles that exist in our world. So many women first tell you, "Motherhood is amazing!", "It's one of the greatest jobs in the world to have!", or, "Being a Mommy is filled with so many wonderful loving times in your life." But how often do you hear that, "Being a mom is f*ckin' hard!", "Going to need that bottle of wine to unload with, once my child goes to bed" or, "How can I be an awesome yet unselfish Mama - who devotes her total life to her child yet still finds the time for a prosperous career, and a loving romance, all at the SAME time?!"

Personally that last question is probably one of the most difficult ones I still struggle with. My fairytale dream of falling deeply in love turned out to be more of a nightmare. Not only was I surprised, and then shocked, to find out that I was suddenly going to become a Mother... totally unexpected at a time in my life that was so NOT planned, but I was also going to have to learn how to live life as a Single Mommy too... totally alone, with full responsibilities for EVERYTHING for my child. My 'Prince Charming', whom I thought loved me wholeheartedly, was actually the 'Big Bad Wolf', hungry for his own freedom instead. How many sacrifices was I going to have to make now as I was forced to become a 'Damsel in Distress' when all I wanted to be was a

'Prosperous Princess' instead? Who was going to be the 'hero' to save me from this evil and help me survive as a 'Single Mommy' now?

Though it happened almost 15 years ago, I can still remember that moment when I first met him... my so-called 'Prince Charming'. I had just finished watching a live concert in a downtown nightclub with one of my favorite 80's bands performing that night. It was such an awesome concert! It was always a fantasy of mine to meet this lead singer in person one day, especially since I used to pretend as a young teen that I was part of his band. It was years before that my sister, my best friend, my first 'boyfriend' and I would often play in the basement of our house, 'rehearsing' with our musical instruments as we pretended we were rock musicians in this Air Band we formed. We would re-enact each hit song - especially from this popular 80's group that we all loved. Never in a million years did I think what I was imagining then, was actually something that was going to come true later on in my life... but in the most unexpected and magical ways.

After that concert ended, I approached the bouncer who was guarding backstage. I had connections there as I worked as a go-go dancer/bartender part-time on weekends and would perform as a back-up dancer/choreographer too. While I was on tour with many pop groups over the years, I also performed on that same stage where I just saw this 80's band perform. I was totally used to being treated as VIP in the entertainment industry. I had a confidence in myself that was very strong, at times a bit egotistical. Actually I hate to admit it, but there were many times that I was very selfish and even a bit conceited during those years. But at least I didn't put up with anyone's sh*t!

Determined to meet this lead singer finally and make my dream come true; as I usually didn't go all 'ga-ga' for someone, I knew I had to meet this rock star once and I would be cool after that. But my excitement turned to disappointment quickly when I looked for him backstage and found out from this dark-haired mystery guy, dressed in black leather, that the lead singer and lead guitarist left the building and were now waiting on the tour bus. I realized then, that this fantasy of mine was not meant to be. However something else was being planned for me... something greater, unknown to me at that time, but coming from a higher power above.

Unexpectedly, this unknown guy was suddenly asking me if I wanted to eat something from the band's food table and then approached me, pushing a strawberry towards my face. As I was about to grab the strawberry with my hand, this guy pressed the fruit against my lips and told me to take a bite of it. Funny how I've watched the cartoon classic Snow White many times before, but I forgot about that scene of the Evil Queen in disguise, feeding the 'poisonous red apple' to her. If only I remembered this moment at that specific time, who knows how different my life could have been?

After the quick bite of the strawberry, this leather bound stranger leaned in towards my face and shockingly KISSED me passionately! How dare he?! I quickly told him off, asking him, "Who the hell do you think you are?!" He told me he was watching me throughout the night while on stage and explained that he was part of the band. Seriously?! I told him I didn't care because I wasn't interested in him, even though he was mysteriously charming. But he obviously started to cast some sort of 'spell' on me. He asked me for my phone number in order to keep in touch, but instead I ended up giving him my email address, thinking how strange it was that I didn't stick to my guns and refuse him completely. Regardless, I really didn't think anything else would come from it.

During the three months that followed, many sweet emails were exchanged between us while he was on tour throughout Europe. Big T would often surprise me with bouquets of a dozen red roses being delivered to my condo, as he would order them online from across the globe. He also surprised me with an airline ticket to fly out to L.A. from Toronto for our first date mini-trip in person! I was finding it really hard not to fall for this guy. He seemed to be doing everything right... just like a 'Prince Charming' would, in order to woo his 'Princess'. How could a girl like me refuse a guy like this?!

What also shocked me was how platonic our 72-hour date really was once I arrived in L.A., and then he surprised me with ANOTHER flight... this time to Las Vegas! He wanted to fly us out to attend a rock concert together, so we could see this other popular rock band perform, which he used to be on tour with. I couldn't believe how ahhhmazing this 'First Date' really was! It was all so magical! But never once did he try to pressure me for sex during this mini-trip, which thankfully I've got to say, was pretty comforting. After the kind of relationships I had before, this 'rock star' here was pretty awesome in comparison. He was a total gentleman in every way! He actually seemed a bit nervous too, which I found was pretty odd - considering who he was.

When I questioned Big T, he told me that he liked me so much and that I was 'hard to get', not like any other girl that he would meet on tour. He confessed that he didn't want to screw things up between us. He wasn't looking for a one-night stand. He wanted a serious relationship... with ME, even though it was going to have to be a long distance romance at first. He surprised me once again, when he told me he was already falling in love with me, ever since he first saw me. I couldn't believe this was actually happening to me! Was this one of my fairytale dreams coming true? I started feeling like I had met 'The One' and was beginning to open myself up with this suave older guy who just happened to be a popular rock musician as well.

During the next three years of our romantic relationship, we managed to share many awesome experiences. The first year, he would fly me out often to stay with him in hot California and even visit me, during the cold weather months here in Ontario. We also met each other's parents within our second and third mini-date trips, and he even told both of our parents that he wanted to marry me one day in the near future. Within the second year, I was invited to go on tour with him and the band across North America which was pretty freakin' awesome, considering the band that he was with happened to have that SAME lead singer that I once had a major crush on so long ago! Not only did I get to meet this singer after all these years, but surprisingly I no longer felt that deep crush I once had for him. Now that I was 'part of the band' as one of the girlfriends, it meant that it really wasn't cool to get all 'ga-ga' over anyone. It kinda felt like I was part of that 'Rock Royalty' clique. Everything around me became so surreal! I truly felt like I was living my OWN rock star dream!

By the third year we decided to look for houses while in California and I was going to make the move out to live with him in the sunny state. I needed to test the waters out there and show him that I could find work as a model, actor, spokesmodel and dancer, which I was already working as in Canada. My goal was to hopefully get a Visa through work instead of having to marry him for that. I really was set on being independent and showing him that I could make it without his financial help because I didn't want to be dependent on him, just in case something happened between us. But what a stupid mistake that was in retrospect, because it totally burned me many years later. When I became a Single Mommy and didn't have him to support me or our child, in any way, he would rub it in my face how independent I wanted to be, so now here was my chance to show it.

Sadly, our fairytale dream started to slowly fade away as we got close to six months of living together. I started to see how my 'Prince Charming' wasn't as supportive of my career goals as I once thought he was. We were playing house and living in the 'castle'- the Manor, together, and I was pursuing my dreams further in the entertainment industry, but without any help from him or his connections. He told me there could only be one 'Rock Star' between us and that it was him and not me. This totally crushed me as I started to see a side to him that wasn't as sexy and charming as the 'Prince' I once thought he was. Now, he was becoming more of a slithery, narcissistic snake instead.

It didn't take long after that to realize this lovely fairytale was not going to end 'happily ever after'. Once I got cast for a lead in a reality TV show, I told Big T I was going to return to Canada so I could sell my condo and come back to start filming. But he told me no girlfriend of his was going to embarrass him like that, so we fought passionately, and then realized we had to break up.

Soon the bad luck seemed to be following me everywhere. Not more than a couple of months later, I found out during a doctor's appointment that I was unexpectedly pregnant while on birth control! How was this even f*ckin' possible?! An emergency ultrasound revealed that I was already 12 weeks pregnant- even though I did NOT have any signs of pregnancy since I was still having my monthly period. I was told to quickly stop taking the Pill and to decide immediately what I was going to do with this 'baby' that was now growing inside of me. I was in total shock! I wasn't planning on becoming a mother, especially when my acting career had a chance of taking off. I was concentrating on my professional goals. Becoming a Mommy was definitely NOT on the radar, nor was it one of my personal goals either.

I gained the courage to call my so-called 'Prince Charming' and told him through tears, "We're pregnant! I'm scared. What are we going to do now?" What he said next, and the decision he made at that time, totally laid out the plan for me during the next 1.5 years. He demanded that I have an abortion because HE didn't want to be a dad right now, even though he told me he missed me very much. Talk about being totally f*cked up! Did he really love me or not?! Why was he playing me like this?! I was so mad, hurt, scared, and a total wreck! I hated myself for being so vulnerable and falling in love with him. But I also had to remember that I had a right to make a decision about my own body and what I was going to do with it.

Again I did not want to be a Mommy, but I knew that I couldn't live with myself if I had an abortion either. I believed in God, I was raised as a Catholic, but I also came from a strict European family background, and being pregnant and single at the same time was not acceptable. My parents were going to kill me! So I prayed instead... for strength, forgiveness, lots of love, and good health for me and this baby that I was now carrying. I decided to make this life-altering decision and give up my love of acting or any other career goals, and instead gain two steady jobs - as a nightclub bartender and as a retail salesperson working close to the end of my pregnancy. I thought I was going to have about two weeks off to relax before the baby came, but instead I ended up giving birth just FOUR DAYS later. I was becoming a Mommy now, whether I was prepared for it or not. The next challenge was whether I was going to do the whole parenthood thing with someone else, or was I going to have to face it all alone and on my own.'

"Whenever you find yourself doubting how far you can go, just remember how far you have come - everything you have faced, the battles you have won, and the fears that you have overcome."
~Unknown

When my son was 1.5 years old, my rock star ex-boyfriend came back on tour in my city and wanted to see me again. This was his third visit back and I've got to say, it was crazy how the chemistry was still there between us, even after everything that had happened. This 'spell' that he must have cast on me was still lingering on, which didn't make it any easier since I gave birth to his first-born child. But it was that third visit that finally changed that passionate connection between us.

Big T surprised me while we were having a bite to eat, right before he was ready to perform on stage. He told me he 'accidently' got someone else pregnant and that he was telling her to have an abortion, too. I couldn't believe my ears! He explained that she was threatening to take him to court for child support as she was refusing to have an abortion. I needed time to quickly process it all. So instead of watching him perform that night, I sat in my car, cried and called my best friend, who was like a brother to me, for some advice. We came to the decision that it was time. I had to find strength and courage within me now, to tell him the secret that I was keeping from him.

After his performance, I finally revealed it, that I NEVER did have that abortion that he thought I had. It was time for him to be shocked instead of me now! I shared with him a picture of our son who was 1.5 years old, and who shared the same dark hair and eyes as he had. I didn't know what to expect would happen next, but I just thought 'expect the unexpected', and so it was.

I reminded him that he made an awful mistake to give up on our baby, but to no avail; my 'Prince Charming' was no longer the same man standing before me. He was now a stranger. Instead of taking responsibilities for his paternal duties, he continued to run away from them and completely disappeared from my life and from his beautiful and precious little son that he chose to, once again, totally ignore and fully neglect. So heart-breaking!

I had to figure out a way to start a child support case against him even though I knew there was also another woman who was pregnant with his second child at the same time. There was so much drama happening, which no soap opera could have ever prepared me for! Talk about putting myself in one of the toughest roles that I've ever had to act! Except in this case, there was NO camera filming and there was NO script to read. Instead, this was the new 'reality show' that I was now living in and I needed to act fast in order to finish strong at the end.

But three months after that, and $5,000 spent with NO formal paperwork filled out, I had to decide how much I was going to have to lose in order to fight him on this international level. I was already running out of money as a Single Mommy. I didn't have enough to go further with this. So instead, I had to put it on my 'To Do List' for another day, when I could start and finish this properly - when the timing was right. I didn't look at myself in this moment as I failed or gave up, but rather as a turning point in my life. I needed to re-focus solely on my son and how I could be the best Mommy AND Daddy to him, which is really what a child needs and deserves. But I also choose not to hide the facts about his dad, especially when he would ask questions about who his dad really was.

Though I decided not to talk about Big T in a negative way - even though I was so disgusted with how he was treating me and our little son, I found I was transforming into the Mama Bear role as I was protecting my little Cub more and more against the Big Bad Wolf himself. All the abuse he was showing us, the disrespect and denial of who we were, was very hurtful, but I knew deep inside, it would be wrong for my son to share in the same hatred against his father that I was feeling. It was important that my son discover his own feelings about his dad, especially once he learned fully all the details of our story.

I needed to put my 'big girl panties' on and become the ever resourceful and hard-working 'Cinderella Mommy' that I had to be. I started working different jobs, while taking care of my son full-time, and also finding time to volunteer weekly to help others over the years, too. This also helped me with my own healing, as I would place my attention on helping someone else rather than being so self-absorbed.

Finding another man to fall deeply in love with was not an option. I didn't want to be so vulnerable with any man again, so I started to build back up the walls around me, like I did long ago. In order to give all my love to my son and make him the number one priority,

I needed to focus my energy on providing my lil' angel with the best that I could... through education, skills and experiences that were available to me. I also needed to sacrifice my own interests/hobbies and career aspirations because I really didn't have the desire to be selfish anymore. It wasn't about me anymore... it was about this little ahhhmazing gift from God! I was so blessed being called his Mama and being chosen as his sole parent, even if I had to do double-duty in his life. This little being truly saved me and made me strong.

"Being a single Mommy - in every sense of the role, is discovering all the strengths you didn't know you had, when dealing with all the fears that you are completely aware of."
~ NMK

As the years passed, I found out there was yet another female who became a 'Baby Mama' with the birth of Big T's third child I knew something needed to be done. My young son and I were NOT going to stay hidden in the dark, left neglected and abused in so many ways, while there were two other children out there... two half-siblings of my son's that he didn't have the pleasure to know. His father - my ex-boyfriend, who was still a rock star, had to finally grow up and start taking some paternal responsibilities for a life that he helped create 10 years ago. I couldn't keep sacrificing all my dreams and goals as a woman and as a mother anymore. I wanted to start living again! But what I found out was I had to first 'die' before I could be 're-born'. So I knew what I had to do... it was time to start this international child support case, but making sure, this time, I saw it fully through to court.

I started preparing myself for battle as this was going to be a war that I needed to fight hard with. I wanted to break free from this 'Damsel in Distress' routine and become the 'Warrior Princess' who I believed I could be! After all, my 'superpower' was... being a Single Mommy! So I became the heroine that I was searching for. I needed to SING and shout as the strong GIRL that I am, and the devoted loving MUM of my wonderful son too, while I remembered to love myself – the ahhhmazing ME. I needed to remember WHO I AM – as the SING GIRL MUM ME that I was meant to live as. I didn't want to be a victim anymore, nor settle living life as a survivor... I was ready to become a WARRIOR now!

Once I started becoming thankful for all that I had, even if it wasn't a lot, I knew the future would become brighter for my son and me once we started attracting it. It was going to take A LOT more sacrifices that anyone could ever prepare me for, but now... I AM READY!

Since I was working as a Montessori Early Childhood Teacher during the week, a bartender and promotions spokesmodel on the weekends, and was volunteering as a leader with Beavers and Cubs and a coach with my son's basketball team, I didn't have the time, or the money, to start legal proceedings. I found out there was ONE way I could do this but it wasn't going to be easy. I would have to commit 'professional suicide' to go on unemployment from teaching, and then eventually live on welfare, in order receive free legal services.

Those 2.5 years of being forced to live on welfare, going to the Food Bank, getting further behind with my bills and falling deeper into debt, was one of the hardest and darkest times of my life. That was less than 2 years ago. But it was also one of the most POWERFUL times for me as well. With my so-called 'Prince Charming' being revealed as the 'Big Bad Wolf' himself, I forced myself to break through the fears that I had, as I knew I couldn't stay scared of him forever. No matter how many moments of anxiety and depression that were developing within me during those impoverished years, I somehow found the strength to carry that sword of hope, faith and belief, that everything was going to get better and better, each and every day. And it actually started to work!

Once the child support court case concluded, just a short time ago, my son's father finally starting paying child support after all these years of abandonment and neglect. But, unfortunately, I found out that according to State child support laws, my son and I could only receive ONE YEAR of retro-active pay instead of the missing 10 YEARS which should have been owed to us. This meant we lost close to a MILLION dollars in back pay which we will never see. Did this mean I 'sacrificed' EVERYTHING for NOTHING? The answer is NO... not at all!

While I may still be dealing with the aftermath of the many sacrifices that I had to make as a mother, I know that this fairytale turned nightmare has shaped me and changed me to become the empowered Warrior Princess that I am presently. My superpowers of being a SING GIRL MUM ME has truly helped me gain my 'butterfly wings', as I am FREE! My son knows who his half-siblings are, he is now present in his dad's thoughts, and we both feel lighter together. I have become the hero that I was searching for all this time... as the loving devoted SING GIRL MUM ME and the strong powerful Warrior Princess too which I was born to be.

MONIQUE KURNATH C.Ht. (aka **NIKKI-MONIQUE**) is a Montessori ECE Teacher, Best-Selling Author, Speaker/Host/Writer, Brand Ambassador and a Well-Fit Specialist within the Holistic Heath of Alternative and Movement Therapies. Her specialities within Wellness and Fitness include: Hypnotherapy, Reiki, PILOXING, ZUMBA KIDS/KIDS JR. and KIDS YOGA. Her passions for Meditation, Chakra Energy, Natural Healing and Volunteering helps encourage others to lead empowering lives. She is the Founder/Creator of a Holistic Childrens Program- POSITIVE POSSE 4 ME, a Movement Therapy- YOGKRA and an active Leader of positive social groups #BMPOWHERD and EMPPACT/PPA. She is the proud #SingGirlMumme of a talented loving son.

Michelle Main

The Main Message: Unveiling the Power Within

"I believe that everything happens for a reason. People change so that you can learn to let go, things go wrong so that you appreciate them when they're right, you believe lies so you eventually learn to trust no one but yourself, and sometimes good things fall apart so better things can fall together."
~Marilyn Monroe

Greg and I are the love story that was never supposed to end. We met in May of 1989. He worked at a Hospital and I was doing my High School Co-Op course in the Admitting Department. I had seen Greg across the crowded cafeteria and asked my friends if they noticed him; the guy with the lab coat, beard and glasses. They said they knew who I was referring to. I then told them that I was going to marry him. They jokingly asked if I was crazy, or on drugs. I denied both and said that I was quite serious that I would marry him. I had never met him. I didn't know his name or where he worked but I knew that I was going to marry him.

One day, I was sitting at my desk typing when he walked by. We smiled and said, "Hi," to each other. I looked down at what I was typing and I had made many errors that needed correcting. I was using the correction button and doesn't he come back through! I blushed and giggled and we smiled at each other again.

I told the women I worked with that I thought he was cute. They knew who he was and called his department to tell him that there was someone here who liked him. They sent someone to come and get me to go meet him. I was young and immature and hid under the desk. They got me to come out and I agreed to go see him. They put me in a little office to wait for him, and they brought "him" in. They brought the wrong Greg! I was so embarrassed! I told the wrong Greg that he was cute but that it wasn't him that I was there to meet. My Greg walked by and I blurted out, "That's him!" The wrong Greg told me his ego was crushed and left. My Greg came in and we basically interviewed each other, eventually agreeing to go out some time. He called in a couple of days and we went to see Roadhouse. We have been together since then, and we thought we always would be.

We have a beautiful son that is now 21 years old. It would be wonderful if we could put this family back together.

During our 27 years of marriage, we have overcome so much. Every time we had to endure something else, we'd say to each other, "If we can overcome this, we can overcome anything. "Maybe we shouldn't have said that. Could we have been calling trouble? There were so many difficult circumstances that we endured and overcame. Who knows? Maybe we will eventually overcome this too. I sure hope so. We still love each other. We talk more than we ever have. I am more grown up and less self-centered. I respect him and care so much for him. I never realized when we were together that we were on the same team. I was too concerned with being right, being hard, and having things my way. If only I had discovered my new way of being throughout our marriage. It would have been so much happier, and more loving. And we never would have broken up.

I have hoped and prayed that he would change his mind and, to this day, I still do.

The 'Talk'

*"Sometimes two people need to fall apart to realize
how much they need to fall back together."*
~Colleen Hoover

I am not known for being able to have difficult conversations. I am a letter writer. This helps me say exactly what I need to say, and then I can have a conversation after the person reads my letter. I gave Greg a letter and sat in my chair. This opened up a horribly difficult conversation, and then those words, "I think you should leave," were said. As asked, I left for a couple of days and returned home to get more things and do my laundry. My husband then left and stayed at a friend's place for ten days. I hated it. I was alone; lonely, sad, scared, and so many other emotions. The pain of him walking out the door was unbearable. I collapsed and cried uncontrollably for what seemed like forever. A piece of me left that day too.

I am the type of person who feels pain, processes it, and then picks myself up and figures out what I need to do next to survive. I honestly had no idea how I was going to do life without Greg. I worked at getting myself even more into a wellness routine than I already was. I was doing Rife treatments 12 hours apart daily for various conditions that I was experiencing. I was meditating, journaling, and being sure to keep my immune system up with vitamins and protein shakes. My dog LuLu was definitely a LIFELINE!

We settled into living separate lives under the same roof, and in the same bed. We were separated, but still loved each other; so naturally, it was hard to not show affection. I would accept his advances, but then he would confirm that we were, in fact, still separated and, my heart would shatter again.

My goal is not to make Greg out to be the bad guy. He is not! In fact, it is the complete opposite! He is a wonderful man who is well educated and has a good job. He is well paid for what he does.

Greg is a wonderful father and went above and beyond to be a good husband. He has endured and dealt with more than anyone should have to. I experienced several accidents that changed me. The pain medication and inactivity more than doubled my weight. My personality changed. I went from being active, happy, fun-loving, and having an amazing sense of humor and zest for life, to being in pain, overweight, unappreciative, miserable, and unable to get around very easily. I was deep into my food addiction, and I forced him to enable me or I would make his life a living hell. He still loved me, and treated me as he always did. I have no idea how, but he did. People would tell me that they could see his love for me in his eyes every time he looked at me. I was the luckiest girl in the world. I had everything that every woman wants and didn't appreciate it.

NLP Course

*"If you have the courage to begin,
you have the courage to succeed."
~David Viscott*

A year prior, I had purchased a course to become an NLP Practitioner. I opened it and was completely overwhelmed. I closed it down and didn't look at it again. This was the perfect time to reopen it. I was sinking fast and thought to myself, "I wonder if that course could help me at least stay afloat?" I mustered up the courage to open it up once more and came to the conclusion that it was definitely worth using to try to save myself. I am so grateful that I did - and that it did. Without it, I don't know how I would have made it through. During the process, I was also able to overcome my food addiction to cake. Recently, I used it to overcome my fast food addiction. I am so relieved that the fast food addiction is a thing of the past. It was deadly! I lived on it because my physical ability was so hindered that I couldn't sit or stand long enough to prepare dinner for my family. Greg accepted this as well, and would pick up dinner on the way home, or I would have it delivered.

Moving Day

"Brave is not saying I have no fear.
It's being terrified and still moving forward."
~Elisa Jimenez

It's April 1st, 2017. MOVING DAY. It was a day I didn't actually think that I would live to see. I went through so many extreme health challenges and emotions during the time when we were separated, but living together. It was so difficult that I actually decided to leave. Going through the last 27 years of my life's possessions was brutal. Sometimes I was on auto pilot, and other times I was an emotional mess. I remember when the photo albums turned up. I took time to go through each one and re-live the memories that were before me. I cried uncontrollably at what I was going to leave behind. They are safe on a closet shelf now, someday to be reopened. I am pretty sure that tears will flow and my heart will ache. I am grateful for the life we had, the memories, and that we have photos to look back on.

Moving Day was horrible. I was in a complete fog, absolutely useless, and unbelievably terrified of what the future had in store for me. I was told not to worry because everything would be set up specifically for me. Well, that plan quickly failed because I ran out of money. It took so much time and money to get through the last 27 years of my life, with the move costing three times more than I figured it would be. If it weren't for my friend Jacqui, I would be still living with loads of boxes in my space. Jacqui has been there for me more than anyone, and I couldn't have done it without her. I have NEVER lived on my own. I went from my childhood home with my parents to my fiancé. I highly recommend that people live alone before they get married or cohabitate. When we are young, there is an excitement of the unknown of living alone. When we're older, there could be fear.

Living alone

*"You never know how strong you are
until being strong is your only choice."
~Bob Marley*

As I mentioned, living alone was new to me. I was afraid to be on my own; every noise, shadow, or flickering light terrified me. I was like a cowering child in a corner. I would stay up so late until my body had no choice but to shut me down to sleep. I was afraid of anything and everything. It's funny because those that know me well told me that if anyone could do this, it was me, and that they weren't worried about me at all. I had my little paranoid/terrified routine before I went bed each night, and I had an alarm system installed the first week for peace of mind.

It has been quite the adventure learning to do things on my own. There's so much that I thought was beyond my ability and yet, I always seem to get it done one way or another. I remember the day I hung my pictures feeling so satisfied because I did them all by myself.

One of my favorite things so far was the day I set up my bathroom. I have so many drawers, shelves and baskets. It's so girly - and all mine, and I love it! Honestly, I didn't think I would love anything about living alone. My own bathroom will be a must from now on! Being responsible for everything is also new to me. Any time I fell on my face, my mom, my husband, or my son was there to save me. Even if it was as simple as picking up my own socks that had fallen on the floor, or putting them on my feet by myself! It didn't matter how badly I screwed up or what I needed, someone would make everything all better.

I needed to get new furniture. I went shopping all by myself and picked out my bed and my sofa set. I picked it out, ordered it and had it delivered. My sofa has been on my vision board for at least seven years. I haven't paid for it yet, but I absolutely love it and I know that it will all work out fine.

I figured that if I needed a new bed, I was going to get one that would benefit me for many years to come. It has a massage feature and is adjustable. It is so comfy and I love it. I discovered that I actually like sleeping alone. I miss my husband terribly, but I now understand why people have separate bedrooms or separate beds.

On My Own

"Everything you want is on the other side of fear."
~Jack Canfield

In a previous book, Live Out Loud, I shared the story of my back surgery where they implemented stainless steel rods into my back because of a deformity, as well as injuries from multiple car accidents, and my Fibromyalgia diagnosis. Physically I was a mess and had no idea of how I was going to be able to fend for myself. The simplest thing like grocery shopping, carrying it all in on my own, and then putting it all away I had not done in so long. I've always had help from my husband and son for anything and everything that I wasn't physically able to do. They always carried everything for me. How could I fix things on my own, reach for things, or pick them up? I had so much fear of the unknown and could not comprehend how I would survive.

Sharing my Home

"Every problem is a gift–without problems we would not grow."
~Tony Robbins

I thought it would be a great idea to open my home to people in need of a place. I figured it would be great to not be alone, cut down on my expenses, and have help for the yard. BIG MISTAKE!!! Alone and scared works out much better than having people in my house who made me want to leave and not come back! They upset me, my LuLu, and my finances. It was a nightmare. My stress levels were through the roof and it was affecting my health. I'm grateful for the experience though, because I was looking to get into real estate investing and this made me realize that it is not for me! It also taught me that it is better to be alone while I work on me. My peace and serenity is more important than the money. It also showed me who was who, and that I needed to become a better judge of character and to not jump into things so easily.

Losing LuLu

"No matter how many years we get with our dogs,
it's never long enough."
~Unknown

LuLu, our family dog of almost 10 years was a life line during the separation. She came and lived with me. I don't think I ever talked to her more than when it was just the two of us in the new place. She followed me everywhere I went and came with me pretty much every time I left the house. She didn't need a leash because she was always by my side. She would shake and cry when she saw me getting ready. I think the separation and move was hard on her. We became inseparable.

One day we noticed that she had a little growth on her left paw about a third of the way up. It grew gradually. I put noni juice on it and it shrunk miraculously. Then all of a sudden, it started to grow rapidly. We made the decision to get it checked and the vet recommended having it removed. LuLu had surgery and was a champ through the recovery.

All of a sudden another growth started on the left side of her chest. This one grew way more rapidly than the one before. The vet had mentioned that this could happen. It grew exponentially. You could see growth over night. It was horrible. Once again, we took her in to get checked. The vet noticed another one coming up on the same paw as before, just a bit above where she had had the other one removed. The vet mentioned the dreaded "C" word and told us we would need to make a decision. My decision was to save my dog! I called a holistic vet and a raw diet was recommended, some spices, coconut oil, and I used a couple of essential oils and ESSIAC as well. Unfortunately, I didn't have enough time to save my LuLu. The tumor was growing day by day. My poor girl. I didn't want to face reality, but I knew the time was coming.

One night, I was headed to a networking meeting and LuLu was with Greg and Carson. Greg called me to tell me that it was time and that he was sorry. The timing of that call was way less than ideal. I wanted to turn around and run to her. Instead, I dried my tears and did what I was scheduled to do. It was difficult to get through the meeting, but getting through difficult seems to be my 'M-O'. I ended up talking about what was bothering me. Clearly I couldn't hide my pain as well as I thought I could. The women in attendance were fabulous, and they gave me hugs and words of kindness.

After the meeting, I drove to my girl and spent hours stroking her head and body and telling her I loved her. My heart broke. How was I going to get through without my girl? She had been my companion, my protection, and my sounding board. She was such a big part of my life.

That night was hell. The tumor started to bleed. I called the emergency vet clinic and they said that due to her size and weight, that she would be okay until morning. I didn't want to sleep. I just wanted to hold my girl, but she didn't want to be held. We 'slept' on the couch that night. In the morning, she was bleeding worse, and, although we already knew what needed to be done, we REALLY knew now; the dreaded decision to put her down. The vet clinic was amazing, but it was still a horrendous experience. When they injected her, she exhaled her last breath in my face and I collapsed on top of her. I didn't want to leave her there all alone. My son literally picked me up off of her and said, "Let's go. This isn't helping you - or Lulu." As a mom I try to be strong for my son, but in that moment, he was the strength, even though he was going through the same thing.

The second worst reason to go to the vet is to pick up a pet's ashes. It rips the wound open again. I sat in the parking lot after I got her urn and cried, and then I cried all the way home. As I write this now I'm bawling my eyes out. I still miss my girl and always will. I am so grateful for the time we shared. In my opinion, it wasn't enough though. LuLu has a special place in my heart where I keep her with me. I often hear her in my room at night. I find her hair suddenly on my page when I am reading. She definitely lets me know she is with me and for that, I am grateful.

Reba

"You'll never get the dog you want.
You'll always get the dog that you need."
~Cesar Milan

I have loved animals for as long as I can remember. I never had any with fur because of my allergies. When Greg and I married, we got a dog and named him Sparkie. He was from a pet store. He was the runt of the litter. We couldn't speak to him when he ate. He would growl and lunge at us. If we reached our arms over the sofa, he would jump up to attack. If we moved our feet on the bed, he would jump in the air and lunge at our faces on the attack. We always knew that when we were ready to start a family that we would likely have to put him down. Sparkie was my dog and the day came when he lunged at my face to attack me. I reached up and caught him and pinned him down. Our tenant heard the commotion and came up and started a fight with me and threatened to sue if Sparkie attacked him or his family. Sparkie would have had to be quarantined for ten days to see what was wrong with him. This would have killed him because he would be away from us. We decided it was time, and we made the decision to put him down.

After Sparkie there was Belle, our first rescue dog. Belle was amazing! She was such a beautiful girl. She thought of our son Carson as her own. She was so protective of me when I was expecting and then when he arrived, she took her security to a whole new level! Belle blessed our lives for over 13 years.

LuLu was our second rescue dog. Following Belle, she had pretty big paws to fill - and she did. She was an amazing dog too! LuLu blessed our lives for almost 10 years. The pain of losing a dog is unbearable to me, as it is for many. I'm a dog person. I don't do life well without one. I didn't last long after losing LuLu. The SPCA had a beautiful dog available. I drove to meet her and knew immediately I wanted her, but there was a family ahead of me. I called to check numerous times but, for some reason, it didn't work out.

Prior to that, I had registered to adopt a pet and got emails of dogs that are available for adoption. There was a link to a dog that reminded me of LuLu. That wasn't necessarily my intention to get a dog that was the same breed or same look as LuLu. The website said she was a Vizla. My friend Jacqui and I drove out to meet "Bella". It was a great visit. She was up on the couch and I asked her if I could sit beside her. She let me sit and pet her. She looked at me with the most loving eyes. Her foster mom said she knew we were a perfect match for each other and "Bella" jumped in the truck to ride to her 'furever' home.

As it turns out "Bella" is a Rhodesian Ridge Back, the same as my LuLu. Bella didn't respond to her name so I needed to come up with a new one. She is a survivor of the Texas hurricane, and her hair is reddish. I love the show Reba and it is based in Texas, so I changed Bella's name to Reba. I said Bella and she ignored me. I said Reba and she looked at me as if to say, "That could work," so I decided Reba it is!

Reba has been here for a while and she seems to have settled right in. Like LuLu, Reba loves truck rides. She also likes my bed and the couch. I've broken her of the bed and I think I might let the couch slide. I get more cuddles this way. Who doesn't love doggie cuddles?!

Creating New Habits

"If you want to move to a new level in your life,
you must break through your comfort zone
and practice doing things that are not comfortable."
~T. Harv Eker

I am learning to live within my means. I am responsible for my financial successes or failures. I was so used to the backup with my husband's paycheck. That isn't an option now.

I have always been messy. Not dirty, MESSY! I've been like a teenager my whole life. I decided that when I went on my own, I was going to work very hard at keeping my abode neat, tidy, peaceful and cheery. I buy myself fresh flowers every week and divide them up throughout the house. I love flowers! How they look, how they smell, and how the make me feel. I am worth it and I deserve it!

My home is surrounded by fast food. I used NLP to take out my fast food addiction and am now eating at home. This helps me live a healthier lifestyle, save money, and be in integrity as a Healthy Lifestyle Coach and Wellness Consultant. I knew better, but couldn't do it before with the food addiction, and physical pain and limitations having such a hold on me.

Living alone is very quiet. I get to decide what I want to do and when I want to do it. No explanation required.

My quiet time consists of many things, depending on my goals or mood. When I want to relax or escape I choose coloring or reading. If I am working on enhancing my health, I do a Rife Treatment and Detox Foot Bath. I love to use Essential Oils. I mix my own blends. I have considered taking an Aromatherapy Course. I've been known to take at least an hour long shower to pamper myself.

I love to learn and I love to read (as long as I am interested in the topic). I take courses in Personal Development or Health on a regular basis. I also attend networking events or seminars. Basically, anywhere I can find like-minded individuals, I AM THERE!

I'm working on me, my business, my home, or my health. No particular order. I do what feels right at the time.

Michelle Main, Party of One.

It's odd going places on my own. Sometimes it's uncomfortable, but I do it anyway and it is usually worth being uncomfortable, working through it, and coming out stronger for it. I quit going out as of August 16th, 2017. I was by myself, dancing at a club, and just stopped all of a sudden and thought to myself, "What the hell am I doing here? I don't belong. It's not fun. I'm surrounded by people who do things that I want no part of." Then I thought to myself, "I'm a published author. Would a published author hang out in a place like this?" Although I don't know if they would or wouldn't - and I don't judge either way, I knew it wasn't a place I wanted to be anymore. It is not serving me and it will not help get me to my goals and dreams.

As I left that night, there were police cars racing to the scene of something. I later found out that someone had been shot around the block from where I was, so I felt it just confirmed that is not the lifestyle that I want to live. I wish I had come to this realization MUCH sooner.

Back to Networking and Meetings

"There are two primary choices in life: to accept conditions as they exist, or accept the responsibility for changing them."
~Denis Waitley, Author and Speaker

Going out on weekends without my husband for the last seven years took its toll. I was no longer working on my business, my goals or dreams, or my family. I was hanging out with people who weren't going to get me to what I had previously been working towards. My self-esteem had taken multiple hits, and I couldn't deal with the lies and betrayals from 'friends' anymore.

In September, I started going back to Business Networking Meetings to look for new tribe members; people, who are like-minded, on a similar path, were supportive and helpful to one another, and chasing their dreams. My morale is way up and I have attracted some wonderful women that I am proud to know and call my tribe. This is my second book. I am networking regularly, meeting with business owners and networking on social media as well. I am an ever-evolving work in progress. I work on my mind, body and spirituality, as well as my home and business.

Without my struggles, I would never have ignited my Inner Warrior. She is a Badass Chick that I seriously underestimated.

I close with this quote because it represents my journey. Maya demonstrates the unknown strength within, without knowing we have it until we have no choice but to unveil it.

"We delight in the beauty of the butterfly, but rarely admit the changes it has gone through to achieve that beauty."
~Maya Angelou

Michelle Main is the Founder of U Can Change Your Life. Specializing in a Healthy Lifestyle, Wellness and Cleanse Coaching. Her passion is helping others Change Their Life. Recently Certified in NLP (Neuro Linguistic Programming), she was able to overcome addiction, release fears and trauma. Michelle is an Entrepreneur, a Philanthropist, and Networker and Master Connector. Due to her love for nature, she is all about natural products, natural health and green products.

Michelle can be booked as a Motivational/Inspirational Speaker. Most importantly, Michelle is a MOM to her beautiful and amazing son Carson.

Pain shapes a woman into a warrior.
~ r.h. Sin

Dr. Ingrid Pichardo Murray

Making Changes... One Step at a Time

One of my earliest memories as a child living in the Dominican Republic (D.R.) was dancing and playing in the rain with my cousins. Running up and down the narrowed passageways and tripping over the uneven pavement were normal to us at the time. We would have the time of our lives just enjoying the cold, crisp rain. Innocently, we didn't worry about tornado warnings, hurricanes, or lightning bolts. We were just feeling free and laughing hard at anything for no reason. I was fortunate enough to live with my paternal grandmother, who I thought was my biological mother. She raised me, along with nine other children in the house. As a child the house and the patio appeared to be gigantic, but now the house is a small modest home with a small front patio, an aluminum roof, and concrete floors. Although the house was small and we were poor, we had the times of our lives.

Now, although we were poor, I was always fed WELL. My parents were already in America so they would send my grandmother money to take care of me. I remember going to the "bodega" (corner convenience store) where I was fed cookies and soft drinks in between meals. On the island eating has always been a big deal. If you could afford it then you were guaranteed to eat three square meals a day. Before my parents left for America they always had money to make sure I was fed. I was such a big baby that I won a healthy baby contest. The prize for winning the contest was more food! I grew up being an obese infant, which led to becoming an obese child, teenager, and then adult. All throughout my childhood I was overfed by everyone in the family. In the Dominican Republic a fat child was somewhat of a sign of good health and fortune. It was kind of big deal. I grew up in a culture that glorified food. Our family gatherings always involved eating lots of Spanish food. Any event turned into a party and food was always the focus. When I would visit my family in New York I would eat dinner in two different households, not only because the food was so good, but also because I did not want to turn their food down. My relationship with food was obviously dysfunctional. I looked like an adult as a teenager, but with a child-like, innocent mentality.

When I immigrated to America, those same Caribbean habits followed me. I would overeat because that was the only thing I knew how to do. We would focus our lives around food. All celebrations involved eating; whether it was a party, a meeting, or an outing. I remember eating fried eggs with french fries for breakfast when we would visit our family in New York. If we were lucky, sometimes we would add some fried hot dogs. Looking back I realize how unhealthy it was to consume all that fat. At the time I did not realize that these choices were unhealthy, or that my eating habits would haunt me in the future. In addition to eating poorly and overeating, I was also shamed for eating because I was an overweight child. I was told that my siblings were thin and I was overweight. My food was portioned because my parents did not want me to become obese. When everyone was finished with their dinner, my job was to clean up, and when I was finished with the kitchen I had to go to the living room to do sit-ups and push-ups. Although I hated the forced exercise sessions, I did them because I respected my parents.

My weight became a daily struggle. What made this fact even more painful was that I had to be reminded of it every day. I was once a prized child; fed well and praised for it in the DR. In America I was constantly told that certain clothes would not look good on me and that those would be the ones that would look good on my much skinnier sister. Although I would not say anything, I believe that the constant comparisons eventually harbored resentment. I found myself being the 'victim' of being overweight. For years I would blame my overeating on my parents and other people. I never wanted to acknowledge the root of the problem. As I became older and wiser, I came to the realization that the reason why I was fat was not because of anyone else. The reason for my overweight status was because of me. It took 23 years of my life to realize that I had the power to take control of my eating habits.

Physical therapy school helped me come to that realization. Learning about the science behind exercise physiology and the complications that come with having high blood pressure and diabetes made me more aware of how our bodies can be harmed and healed. I had a major realization that impacted my life. I realized that I was one of only two overweight people in my physical therapy class of 45 people. I asked myself if others in the class were making good grades like me, how come they found time to exercise? At that moment, I stopped being 'the victim'. I decided that it was time for me to be accountable for my decisions. I decided to make small consistent changes to my lifestyle and diet. I began by implementing the information that I was learning in class into changing my lifestyle habits. Making small consistent changes in my diet and in my activity level made me establish a different relationship with food. I realized that if other students could make good grades like me AND work out, well, then I could do it too. At the beginning of physical therapy school, I was wearing size 14; by the end of school I was wearing size 6. It took me over two years, but I lost 40 pounds the right way. I kept the extra weight off for over ten years.

Amazingly enough, even though the weight had come off, my mental state was still 'fat'. I found myself still wearing my oversized bras; it took my sisters to tell me that I needed to go shopping for new ones that fit my new body. I didn't see it for myself for a long time. After I had lost the weight, I felt more confident. I wanted to go shopping, go out dancing and maintain my attendance at the gym. Making the commitment to lose weight and stay fit did not only help me in my personal life, but it also helped me become a better healthcare professional. One of the reasons for me working so hard to reach my weight loss goals was to set a good example for the patients that I served. I did not want to be that physical therapist that was not practicing what she preached. If I was asking my patients to lead a life of good health and wellness then I needed to do the same. Patient education was the hallmark of my therapy sessions. In physical therapy school, we were taught to explain health care issues to our patients and I was passionate about that. I was especially dedicated to discussing weight loss as part of the patients' therapy sessions. I realized that losing weight was the secret to living a healthy lifestyle.

Fast forward about twenty years after I lost weight by eating small, frequent meals and exercising, I became a married woman with one child and a million responsibilities. I started spiraling down the old path of unhealthy eating. I was walking, and I tried to go to the gym, but, unfortunately, either I just was not consistent enough or the extra years were taking a toll on my metabolism because I was not seeing a huge difference. I honestly tried to work out. The first thing I did was join a boot camp after I had the baby. I wanted my body back so I went outside of my comfort zone and showed up at 6 a.m. to work out in a park at least three times a week. It was amazing how hard it was for me to get back into the exercise routine. Doing a simple sit up was hard because my abdominal muscles were mush. I did gain some strength, but it was difficult to see any significant changes on the scale.

Life responsibilities took over my schedule. I felt like it was not a priority to exercise every day like I did when I was in my twenties. I was a married mom now with many things to do each day; I had other priorities that made me put myself on the back burner of the house's priority list. Riddled with bills and a need to make money just to survive was my life now. Working out and taking care of my body was not a big priority.

It was also getting harder to exercise because I started developing symptoms of asthma during the pregnancy. I was seriously in denial. How could a health-conscious health care professional like me succumb to illness? In my mind I was not suffering from a 'breathing disorder', I just used the inhaler every so often. I just carried it around with me for PRN (as needed) use. I was on a roll with ignoring my needs and I poured myself out for others. I became a professor at the university where I was responsible for up to 120 students. That job was perfect for me because I had so many more people that I could 'help' so I wouldn't have to deal with my own issues. I became good at coming up with excuses about not exercising, not taking days off, and not taking care of myself. I was carrying most of the financial weight of the house. I was working two full-time jobs, working on two doctorates, and taking care of my daughter and husband whenever I had time. There was no room for me. I was a work horse who had to perform without taking a break. Whether I was feeling well or ill, it did not matter. The only thing that mattered was the fact that I was making money to sustain the household.

One day, my body couldn't take it any longer. The albuterol breathing treatments were not working. I was so desperate to breathe that I took my shirt off. It didn't help, and then I wondered where I would find the energy to be able to put it back on again. The 30 minutes that took the ambulance to arrive to my house seemed like hours. Finally, the crew arrived, but I could not believe that they expected me to walk down the stairs. Amazingly made myself walk down the stairs and they were waiting to put me on the gurney. I will never forget the looks on my husband's and daughter's faces when they wheeled me out of the house. When

I was sitting in the back of the ambulance the oxygen mask was not helping me and I began asking the paramedics to give me epi (epinephrine) because I could not breathe. The next thing they did was put in an IV line in my arm and I did not wake up until two days later. I later learned that I was intubated due to respiratory distress and they were giving my lungs a chance to rest.

After my hospital stay, I finally opened my eyes. I realized that all the money, titles, degrees, and jobs were not going to help me achieve my health goals. I needed to stop with the laziness and the excuses. I decided to be proactive and take responsibility for my health. Never do I ever want for my daughter to feel as if she was going to lose her mommy for a senseless reason. Asthma is a treatable disease. I needed to make time for my doctor appointments. I needed to take the proper steps to take control of my health. I needed to take my asthma meds so that I could breathe and optimize my work outs. If you can't breathe, you can't even walk around the block.

Slowly but surely I started walking around the block. I started setting goals to reach my 10,000 fitness tracker steps. Walking was a small accomplishment, but it gave me hope. I continued to reach my step goals until I began moving outside of my comfort zone. I decided to attend a high intensity boot camp group on Sundays. I did the best I could. I realized that I was always the last one to finish all the exercises, but I tried to focus on what my body could do. I preferred to do the exercises correctly instead of rushing through them and taking the chance of getting hurt. I almost dreaded going because for a long time people would ask me if it was my first time attending the class. I would tell them that I had been there before, but I was just trying to get used to it. Unfortunately, I was not consistent enough for them to even remember that I had been there before. I learned to become more consistent and now I have noticed a difference in my strength, flexibility, and endurance. I can keep up with the others as the instructor continues to challenge us every day. I am proud to say that I am getting my body back. The funny thing is that now I want to go to the gym. I don't want to stop because, not only do I notice a positive difference in my body, but I also notice a positive difference in my mindset. When I am at the gym and I feel challenged with an exercise, I work on my mental focusing abilities. I focus on an object and learn to work through the pain that is telling me to stop or take a break. I figure that if I put the weight down to rest, then I must work twice as hard to pick it back up and start again. Once I am finished with my workout I feel a sense of accomplishment that makes me feel proud and excited. I leave the gym with more energy, more stamina, and more focus to tackle my daily responsibilities.

I decided to no longer play the victim. I made the conscious decision to learn how to be tenacious. Tenacity means being flexible but strong. I had to be both to come out strong in the game of life. I know one thing for sure; my journey is not over. I will continue to work day and night to find that balance that I seek. It is not easy. Life is a struggle and sometimes you must do things that you do not 'feel' like doing. I have learned to adopt the mantra of "80% of success is showing up." I am living proof of that phrase. I may not 'feel' like going to the gym, but once I make it there and finish my workout, I say to myself, "Wow, I did it... and it feels good."

Changing my life habits to eating right, working out, taking care of my hair, skin and nails makes me happy. I am all about setting myself up for success by taking care of me before I take care of everyone else. I am learning the fine art of delegating and educating my family members to take care of themselves. I dive in to do things for them when I find that it is prudent. If I feel like doing something for them I do, but I am not doing anybody any favors if I kill myself. I won't be the 'somebody' who does everything for everybody anymore. The most important pearl I have learned from this life experience is that I needed to curtail my life in a way where I maximized my "ME" time and minimize my busy time. I found a job where I could work from home one day and work evenings three days a week in the hospital. The days I work are consistent, for the most part, so I can plan to exercise and take care of household duties on the other days. Since I have been working out in the gym, I am not only feeling strong on the outside, but I am also feeling strong on the inside. This inner and outer strength has enabled me to start sharing my experience and story on my time off. I decided to become an empowerment coach that teaches women how to eat properly, exercise, and take care of themselves. The goal is to teach women that they can be powerful by making healthy lifestyle choices. Women have the power to make healthy food choices, manage their time effectively, and strike the balance that they need to lead a purposeful life.

Dr. Ingrid Pichardo Murray is a physical therapist and a physician assistant who has over 20 years of experience in the healthcare field. She has been a practicing physician assistant for the past 16 years and has had the opportunity to work in the field of pediatrics, orthopedics, internal medicine, emergency medicine and academia. Throughout her professorship tenure, she was promoted to an administrative role with the university. She has found that she enjoys teaching people about medicine and about optimizing their potential to reach high levels of success. Currently, she is a mindset transformational coach that empowers women to take care of themselves first. By making healthy lifestyle choices, she believes that women can achieve anything.

Lisa Rizzo

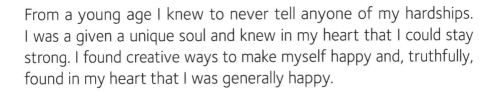

Walking With Spirit

From a young age I knew to never tell anyone of my hardships. I was a given a unique soul and knew in my heart that I could stay strong. I found creative ways to make myself happy and, truthfully, found in my heart that I was generally happy.

Born and raised by a single mother to five children, I was for the most part alone, as most of my siblings were out on their own by the time I was born. My mother didn't have a job so the money that would come in barely covered our bills. She struggled to keep a roof over our heads and food on the table. Life was uncertain. Most of the time my main meal was provided by the school lunch program. We often didn't have food at home. My clothes were from the Salvation Army. (I actually didn't mind this, though, because I always liked to put my own look and spin on my outfits.) There were many holidays that came and went without a gift. If my mother did put a Christmas tree up that was good enough for me. I loved her very much and without judgment.

I spent much of my time alone in my room. I would talk to, and listen to, the whispers of people I could not see. One day I asked, "Who are you? Why can't I see you?" That same night after asking those questions as I was sitting on my bed reading a book, I felt a presence in the room. I looked up and there was a shadow of a woman standing at the end of my bed. I wasn't sure what I was looking at. She had long white hair and a long white dress, and blue eyes like the sky. I asked, "Who are you?" I wasn't scared. I felt so curious to finally be able to see and speak to a ghost. For some reason I was always curious about the dead. I wondered where people's souls went to after this life.

She looked at me with a smile on her face and put her hand out for me to grab it. Without fear, I put my hand out to grab hers and my hand went right through. She abruptly disappeared. I felt a sad longing for some reason, and asked her to come back. She didn't that night. I went to sleep not even thinking anything about how unusual my experience was that evening.

I had opened the door to another world. I started receiving visits from the spirit world on a regular basis. In this new world I found offered a place of belonging and comfort. I knew instinctively in my soul that I was safe. It was also a knowing that I had been in this place before. I enjoyed each experience and looked forward to spending time with the spirit world.

I spent every day with two angels which I call guides. I knew they were sent to me to help me walk through life so that I didn't feel alone. There was a knowing within me that this life was going to be a journey. I believe we all walk this earth with spirit guides (Angels from your creator) but most don't recognize their presence.

I began to realize that what I saw, no one else could see. I started to see spirits walking amongst me all the time. It became a part of my life that I just accepted. My spirit guides started to show me that something was going to happen before it would occur. One day, still very young, I was playing hopscotch with my niece. She suddenly ran out onto the road, as she had seen a kitten on the other side. I ran out after her, pushed her out of the way as an approaching car slammed on its brakes. I was looking straight at the headlights of this car. The feeling of complete peace came over me, due to a déjà vu moment before it was going to take place. I inherently knew that I was going to be safe. I always trusted my spirit guides. My mother frantically questioned why I ran into the road after her. I had no answer for her as I didn't think she would understand my visions, so I kept them to myself. I felt so content inside that I didn't think twice to help another human being. It was without question when it came from the spirit.

At a young age I moved out, worked two jobs and had my own place. In my spare time I studied and learned from my elders and spirit walkers all that I would need to know in this lifetime. I felt that my purpose was going to come to me as time went on. I was always told by others, that I was an old soul, looking for answers to many questions. I believed that all the answers would come in time, even though there were many times in my life I had wanted to give up. I would just pick myself up and continue to walk forward. My spirit guides started to show me more and more of the spirit world.

I would often sit in my room and write songs for hours. All the while, never knowing what I was really writing about or who I was going to sing them to. But I sat on my front porch and sang to the sky. My front porch was on the second floor of an upstairs apartment. I couldn't see people down on the street. On one of those times as I sat on that porch, singing my heart out, it was pouring rain. My guides told me to stand up and look over the railing, so I did. Looking over, there were seven people standing in the rain listening to me sing. I was embarrassed as they started to clap their hands, and I ran in the house and hid in my room.

I cowered, overwhelmed and crying, and my guides said to me, "You are loved and gifted. You are a chosen one." I was confused being told that I was loved because I didn't understand the feeling of love. Gifted; what does that mean? Chosen One? This experience was the first time I wasn't comfortable with spirits. I felt empty inside, confused and frustrated. I was comfortable just being a part of the spirit world and helping as many people as I could along the way. I didn't have much time to think about myself at this point of my life, nor have I for most of my life.

The moment I learned how to love myself, however, everything in my life all came together with beautiful purpose. I was moving with the universe. All I needed to do was believe with faith that all things happen for a reason, and that life is only the beginning.

For the first time in my life I asked my creator to send me someone that would love me for all that I am. That summer I met my soul mate. I couldn't have become the woman I truly wanted to be without having the unconditional love and support he gave me. This journey, walking with spirit, but functioning in a 'normal life' takes a lot of balance, but is one that continues to always inspire me.

I didn't know how to control when I was open or closed to the things around me. I would often wake up at night screaming because I would have people, as spirit, sitting at the end of my bed, or ghost children running up and down the stairs. Sometimes my bed would feel like it was on fire because I was feeling or seeing things that the spirits went through before their passing. I felt the deep concern my husband had because he didn't know how to help me.

When you are open to the other side, called the realm, you don't know what or who you are dealing with at any point. Just as in life, there are good people and bad people; the same is true in the spirit world. There are good souls and bad souls. As time went on, I realized that when I feared the bad spirits, I gave them the energy to take from me. They would come after me trying, in any way, to break my spirit in keeping the faith in my creator.

I know what you are thinking. 'Why didn't your guides help you when you were dealing with dark spirits?' They did, but as guides they wanted me to grow into my purpose and start facing head on what I was seeing, smelling, and feeling. I had to learn that I was in control. All spirits are on the other side, and I am alive. I learned to control my emotions by balancing both sides. Even though I could see them walking around me every day, I didn't give them energy to connect with me.

My guides were always teaching me lessons within the spiritual world. By the time I was in my 30's, I was putting together all the pieces in my life and started to embrace my purpose. Going through so many heartaches, disappointments, abuse, and abandonment feelings in my home-life growing up was teaching me that I would be able to not only share my journey with thousands, but to also bring many people peace from their loved ones on the other side.

Walking with spirit constantly has many challenges. For starters, I'm never alone. There are always spirits walking around me and wanting to talk to me. It sounds like being at a big party with everyone talking over each other. All the stories are different. It is loud. And I am trying to NOT hear everyone's story or conversation taking place at the same moment, but trying to focus, center my ground, and keep the balance. My party never ends and never sleeps. As long as the spirit world sees my light around me they know that I can see them and they will do or say anything to get my attention. I don't live a normal life. I see the same things you see in your day-to-day life except I'm the only one that can see and hear everything from this world and beyond death. It's like watching old movies, everyone is in black-and-white, and layered on top of my full color reality. Imagine how bizarre that is to see. I would see the house décor as it used to be, not how it is now. I could walk down a street and see people from all eras walking with me.

Normal childhood experiences were spattered with spirit encounters. When I was younger, there was an old home that my friend lived in down the street from me. One night my mother let me spend the night over at my friend's house. The parents went out and left us home to listen to records. All of a sudden the doors from the living room to the dining room started to open and close on their own. The record player started to skip. I knew that something in that house was trying to get my attention. My girlfriend was scared and called her parents. While she was doing that, I decided to walk around the house. When I began to walk up the stairs to the second floor, the attic door started to open.

Proceeding cautiously, I walked up the attic stairs. When I got to the top, I saw a man hanging from a rope. I ran downstairs. By that time my girlfriend's parents were home, and my mother and the police were there. The police looked throughout the house and didn't find anything unusual. The doors and windows were locked. I looked at my mother and said, "I saw a man hanging in the attic!" She looked at me like I was crazy. One of the officers had overheard what I said, and asked me what I saw. I repeated my finding in the attic. The officer looked at my mother and said, "I don't know how she would know, but there was a man that lived in this house years ago and hung himself in the attic." This wasn't public knowledge. Unlike the sensational headlines now, back then when somebody took their life it was kept private. This was another instance that proved my connection to the realm was real.

Being Lisa and walking with spirit can also be very difficult to have true friends. I can instantly read intentions, and I am brutally honest - with no filter. Sometimes it is really tough to tell someone you care about that the relationship they are in is going to end, or they're going to lose their job. Or at times they are going to lose a loved one. Either way, I'm left with the pain of knowing what's to come and knowing that there's nothing I can do to change it. I love and care unconditionally. I would love to know what it's like NOT to see things coming, but, at the same time, it would drive me crazy not to know because I've had this gift for so long. Like anything in life for me, I've just learned how to balance the gift I was given in order to live the life I want to live.

When I get up in the morning I have gratitude first and foremost. Second, I put it out to the universe and to the spiritual realm what my day looks like to me. I will address who I want to speak to from here and beyond. My relationship with the spirit world is one that can be so rewarding on one hand, and on the other hand, can make me feel very consumed and tired.

I am able to connect with the universe and all it has to offer. It is important for all of us to connect on a level where we are all equal, and for the next generation after us to have heard our stories and our journeys. We, the universe, understand that everything here and beyond moves together. We are a part of the New World. It has already begun. We are learning by empowering one another in a positive way that we move together in the universe and create our destiny, living our journeys together. I learned that, not only was I serving in a positive way throughout my life, but I was doing it without wanting something in return. It was just naturally within me.

Everything I have put into place in the last five years was sent out to the universe. Everything I said would happen has taken place. I have spent over 30 years of my life serving my purpose. Even though it can be a difficult balance, each and every act of kindness that I was able to share and give to others always filled my heart and soul. I have been honored to be a part of each and every soul I was able to touch in some way.

One Christmas Eve, I got a call from a client that asked me to come out to her home that evening. Of course I said it was Christmas Eve and I had plans with my family. In her voice, however, I heard her desperation to have closure for her sister. She told me that her family had brought her sister home from the hospital to be with her family for Christmas, they didn't expect her to make it much longer. So I asked my guides what to do. I heard this short phrase, "You are one of the chosen ones." I couldn't believe what I was hearing, nor did I feel I deserved that title. Like always, feeling unworthy of this title, I needed to respond to honor my spirit guides. So I took my daughter and son to this family's home with me that night.

When I got to there, the house was full of people. I walked in to find this woman on her bed in the living room with her family standing around her. She was so loved, so very frail, and she couldn't speak.

I grabbed her hand and told her that she could talk through me if there was anything that needed to be done or to be said. Within a few minutes she was telling me who each and every person was in the room around her. And I was pointing to each and every person and telling them who they were to her and what her wishes were. Needless to say her family was amazed that I could recite all their names and details of their life through this dying woman who was not speaking. She told me to tell her sister, who was standing beside her, that she made all her wishes come true. She had made a will before she died. She knew her time was coming and she made sure she didn't miss a thing or anyone in that will. She identified who was going to get what, and how she wanted her funeral to be. I was speaking for her and her family couldn't believe all that I knew, even down to her mother being upstairs in the bedroom that evening, and knowing that she had on the earrings that she gave their mother in her will. She identified her one younger son in the house, but also told me that one of her sons did not want to be there when she passed. She asked me to please have someone go get this second son. He was called by family and came to say goodbye as she requested. So I continued on, like I always do, to complete her wishes, and relay all her details. The family was overwhelmed, filled with both joy and sadness.

But this client wasn't done with me. I heard her say, "You were in my dreams last night. Who are you? And what the f*** are you doing here?" I couldn't suppress a little giggle. Her sister asked, "What did she say!?" I said, "Don't worry, it's okay. I don't think I want to say aloud what she said to everyone on Christmas Eve." The whole family begged to know. When I told them they laughed and said that was their sister; outspoken and determined! She passed away two hours after I had left, with full peace.

How did I feel? What were my emotions on this Christmas Eve night? In that room, filled with love, I was reminded how precious life is and that it should never be taken for granted.

I continue to move forward no matter who, or what, tries to get in my way. I have had many lessons to learn. I am forever learning how important it is to be happy and healthy and to never give up on your dreams; they are mine to conquer. I know before I came into this world I had a specific purpose, but the creator never promised me an easy journey. I am forever blessed. Most gifted people say, at one point or another in their lifetime, that their guides move on when their work is completed here on earth. The spirit world always will be a great part of my soul and my spirit that allows me to continue in my journey, to grow and to fulfill my purpose.

I've reached a time in my life where there's been a great shift happening. Over the past couple of years I've been sick and the doctors can't seem to find the source of my illness. I reached out to many of my friends that are naturopathic doctors, but nothing seemed to help. I really don't want to keep asking. I am not one to talk about what is going on in my life, or share my problems with others. I've always tried to keep things very positive for everyone. Perhaps because I carry the worry and unfinished business of the spirt world I don't want others to worry about me. It weighs too heavy on my heart. It finally came to me that I needed to detox and heal myself from all the years of consuming others' pain, sickness, drama, and, yes, sometimes the darkness within.

I've been blessed to be born with native Indian blood. I've always respected my native Indian culture. I knew it was time to return to my people for healing. I didn't realize, however, how far away from it I was. I looked at my life and all the wonderful accomplishments. I forgot one basic rule in our native culture. 'Keep it simple.' I started to attend many healing circles. I was stunned by the simple observation of one of my elder mothers when she asked, "Lisa, do you speak to every person that you see walking down the street?" I replied, "No." Elder mother continued, "Do you speak to your neighbors every time you see them?" I said, "No." Elder mother then said, "Why do you feel the need to speak to all those from the spirit world?" The elder mother told me it was time for me to rest. That my fire has been burning bright for a long time. That it was okay to now become the amber in the fire. I didn't have to serve anymore. I must return to myself and set forth a new journey in my next chapter.

I could not believe how my elder mother's words resonated with me. I was burning both ends of the candle and I was running out of energy and life within. I knew then that at some point in my life I took a turn down the wrong path; not that I was doing something I didn't love, but I had forgotten how to keep the balance. I spent most of my life healing and putting spirits to rest, and I had totally forgotten about myself. This was all new to me. I have always put others before myself. My family and my closest friends would tell me that all the time. Not only was I not listening to the people that loved me, but I also wasn't listening to myself. This was very hard for me as I always felt deep down that if I didn't make others happy, both here and beyond, that I wasn't serving my purpose. I was so wrong. Here I was sharing with everyone how important it was to unconditionally love themselves first, yet I was not doing the same for myself.

I've come full-circle, and now it's about my healing in my new beginnings for the next chapter of my life.

I call this next chapter the 'Warrior Within'. I spend a lot of time now with my family, sharing with them our native culture. I am also connecting and healing with my ancestors, and returning to the basics of spirituality and connecting to Mother Earth. I bought land in the country with many trees. I spend hours sitting with the trees and listening to my ancestors speak, and I feel the water that flows under my feet. This past year I have begun heal. I had a custom powwow drum made for my family. I love to play it to produce an overwhelming feeling of connection to our ancestors and to each other. I also love having an evening bonfire on the property for sharing stories and healing. My elder mother told me, "The best stories are the ones that are told in person, for the ones that are truly listening will get the lesson. For those that missed the lesson, it wasn't theirs to receive on that day."

I now live in the mindset of 'keeping it simple'; what doesn't feed my soul I let go. The ones that seek their true selves are the ones that will walk with you through this next journey. My family and I have always called ourselves the 'Wolf Pack', meaning we are forever connected and we never let anyone walk alone. We are as one.

It may seem odd that I found my inner warrior in rest, when I was always so driven to serve others. I am still very much in touch with my spirit world. But the warrior has to stop feeding the ego. The warrior does not have anything to prove. His gifts may be given to him in abundance, but the warrior must not give away, or take, more than is needed, and in doing so, is truly giving and sharing of self. The warrior is showing and teaching his people how important it is for our future descendants and our Mother Earth that moving with the flow of the river is the way to live. We have a time to burn bright, and a time to be the amber in the fire. To forever be thankful that we are able to wake up to the sun on our face and to listen to the whispers in the winds that tell us we are alive. I connect with the other realm when I want to, and not out of obligation.

I am in the time of great peace and it has humbled me. I have made mistakes, and will continue to be far from perfect. But I will not waste any more time or energy on things or people that don't feed my soul. My pleasing ego is dying. I will now share my native culture with our healing circles, powwows, and simply positive energy flow to all that are ready to heal. I am enjoying being the amber in the fire and taking in all that mother earth has provided; flowing with the universe and connecting with the souls I was meant to connect with.

My job here on earth continues to evolve. The path I have now chosen is to work less and play more, and enjoy my family and friends. So ignite the warrior within! I will meet you there. No journey is too small, or too big, to conquer. Always remember to continue to put your dreams out into the Universe because it does listen. Always love yourself as you want others to love you. As long as you keep the light glowing within you, there will always be angels beyond death. Angels that walk among us will always guide you in the right direction if you do not fear them. I am the warrior within. I am the leader of my Wolf Pack. I exemplify love, respect, and honor.

Lisa Rizzo is a businesswoman, mother, wife and full-time spiritual medium. She lives in Toronto Canada, with her wonderful husband and three children. She loves to connect with as many souls here on earth and beyond. She loves to write and share her journey with others, so others maybe empowered to write their stories. Life is a journey we all can share together.

Carol Starr Taylor

The Art of Reinvention

"She stood in the storm and when the wind didn't blow her away, she adjusted her sails."
~Elizabeth Edwards

I longed for that safety net. You know that feeling of security, support, unconditional love, and peace? Well, that was foreign to me. The more I wanted it and tried to seek it out, the deeper in despair I fell. Clearly, the fairytale wasn't in my future. Funny, I always thought I was invisible - or perhaps that was a wish, the jury is still out on that one. Invisible in voice, for sure, however, I certainly wasn't invisible to my abusers - just a target.

Growing up in a household of physical, verbal and emotional abuse took its toll. It had been an albatross setting the tone that truly affected my entire life. That vicious cycle. I exhibited patterns of behavior that are synonymous with Victims. Jumping from fire to firestorm seemed to be my normal. The neediness, the people pleasing, the desire to be loved so badly, even though I felt unlovable, all leading me to make certain choices that left me personally depleted in every aspect of the word.

The wrath of my father and the disdain of my mother created an insecure, fearful, and rebellious child. Still I was that feisty little girl, trying to assert my opinions even though I knew the outcome. Being the eldest, I took the brunt of it. No matter what I did, I felt I couldn't do anything right in their eyes, which gave me the sense that I was worthless in my own.

Never did I have that feeling of being safe. The house of horrors was our family secret. To the outside world, we were this beautiful, happy, well known and successful family. Looks are deceiving. The byproduct, of course, is that I learned to keep my mouth shut and to wear my mask to the outside world. But as I shut my eyes, still to this day, I can feel the chilling fear of being physically beaten and emotionally raped of all who I was and wanted to be.

All throughout my childhood and youth, being trapped, I had wanted to escape. Oh, I had so many plans to run away, but far too afraid to ever execute them. I was a victim of my circumstances; that was all I knew. I learned to be the victim and became an expert at it. But what I wanted most of all in the world was to be loved. I trusted people, gave all of myself to receive the love I lacked, in return. That really never came at that time, at least not authentically, and when it did, it showed up in events too far and few between.

The deep rooted desire for unconditional love and acceptance led to my FIRST major life faux pas (indicating that there were others in the future) marrying a man 10 years my senior, whom I didn't love, at the age of 17. He professed his undying love for me, promised me security and a life of freedom and bliss. My first thought: escape. Upon reaching the decision to actually go through with it, my reasoning (if you call it that), was that I truly believed no one else would ever find me attractive, and I didn't want to end up in my life alone. My parents signed the legal papers as I was underage, and released me to this man. What could possibly go wrong?

I experienced womanhood at the hands of this man, legally my husband, but my innocence was shattered, as he completely violated me. Today, yes, we call that rape. As I write this, knowing all I know, tears fill my eyes, remembering and reliving that time. I feel so terribly sad for her... for me.

My life swirled into a rollercoaster over the next 8 1/2 months. He was a pathological liar, I visited him in a mental institution, and he took 2 attempts on my life. I finally divorced at the age of eighteen.

I am no stranger to rock bottom. Oh, I know it well. It has become that familiar place albeit physically, emotionally, spiritually, and financially. Each time, although the one-two punch seemed to blindside me, I still came back up as if I was taunting life and saying, "Is that all you got? Bring it on!"

The battle scars on the outside have faded but the ones on the inside left deep impressions that needed mending. I have always been different, never really part of any one particular 'tribe'. I have always been the Black Sheep in my family and felt that others always saw me that way, too. Spending years being a chameleon and trying to fit in, and really never achieving it, I now understood that to save myself, momentous change and action needed to happen.

The Hunter

The decision to leave my 20+ year marriage and the life I had known had been a complete shakeup, not only for me, but to my ex-husband, children and the gossip-mongering community.

Fresh out of the gate, after making those drastic changes and moves in my personal life, I sprinted to what I thought was empowerment. I had new hot body after shedding 60 pounds, new-found freedom I have never experienced before, and an exuberant 'I'm in charge of myself' attitude; set the stage as The Hunter.

Admittedly, yes, I was THAT girl; the alluring, doe-eyed, pouty- lipped, full cleavage girl on social media and online dating sites. You know the type, gathering potential suitors, seeking validation outside of myself from men, as the attention fed my hunger for acceptance.

For the first time in my life, I felt in charge. Released from the cage, I enthusiastically explored my new terrain, conquered my fears, discovered new heights and took no prisoners. The more I experienced however, the emptier I felt inside of myself. My body was a shell to be used, but the empowerment I mined turned out to be 'fool's gold'. Little did I know that I was in fact being 'The Hunted'; yet, another faux pas.

When you play with fire you get burned. And that I did. I was finding myself in situations with people that saw my vulnerable side and went in for the kill. The characters I encountered had been the most unsavory. They projected fine outward appearances, but were wolves adorned in designer sheep's clothing; liars, cheaters, game players, and sociopaths on the prowl, looking for a girl like me.

I lost myself once again. This time sinking even deeper to that rock bottom lead to a soul searching quest. I realized that I wasn't empowered at all. I was fooling myself to believe that I was. What I discovered was to actually BE empowered is the 'perfect trifecta'; Self Love + Self Worth + Self Esteem = Empowerment. This, in fact, turned out to be an extremely pivotal discovery in my own personal evolution.

The Shield

Seeking refuge from being hurt, sinking yet again while licking my fresh wounds, developed my next phase of reinvention; The Shield.

Completely in the headspace of living in my masculine energy, I retreated to becoming the Teflon Shield. I didn't have any girlfriends at all. The last one had been the final gauntlet, the betrayer. Now I felt completely alone, not really trusting anyone, male or female. I knew realistically that I'm not an island, but I had to protect myself from getting hurt and sinking again. The Shield allowed me to venture out cautiously, without being vulnerable. The problem, of course, that I faced was that, as with any mask or Shield, real authentic connections are impossible to encounter. Superficial, casual and meaningless relationships manifested, in which I became the main culprit. Too wrapped up protecting myself, I realized that this was more isolating than anything I had ever experienced before. A self-imposed banishment.

As with the law of attraction, the energy you emit, you attract. And that I did. Unfortunately, what I attracted was what seemed like a stream of lack luster friendships, poor communicators, self-centered, self-absorbed people where I completely felt like the outsider once again. It just wasn't Me.

I realized that the Shield needed to come down and I had to call a truce on myself. The battle I had been having within provided an epiphany. I realized that, in fact, I was actually fighting against my true nature— to love. I needed to raise that white flag. Honestly, I was terrified. How can I leave myself unguarded? I have had so many failures - personally and professionally, heartache and pain. How DO I protect myself?

The Warrior

I think I was just tired of fighting with myself, completely lost, and feeling like I wanted to die. After years of trials, triumphs, and then further battles, I felt completely broken. Utterly unable to believe that my life had any meaning I was stuck in the 'Why Me?' mentality.

I sat in my car, crying. Although that was a usual thing, this particular day turned out to be quite different. I had allowed myself to trust, let my guard down just a little bit, and my whole life came crashing down around me as a result. I was angry at myself for letting that happen yet again. I hit rock bottom, this time face first, with no one, and nowhere to turn. I just didn't want to deal with it any longer.

Alone. Yes, once again, I was alone. My thoughts were all jumbled together. I was thinking of my children, feeling that they would be better off had I not lived any longer. Other than them, what impact had I really made on anyone, anyway? Sure, I tried to always live with good intention, honesty and integrity just to be squashed to the ground each and every time. I failed my kids - and I failed myself. Everything I touched turned to shit. What's the point of being a good person?

I opened the mirror on my driver side visor and looked at my mascara stained face and swollen eyes, prompting me to wipe away the tears. Looking straight into my own eyes I asked myself out loud, "God, what happened to you?" Then looking away from the mirror, gazing through the window, seeing nothing in particular, and seeing everything at the same time, I had THAT moment.

A surge of energy filled my entire being with this unexplainable feeling of calm and clarity; true inspiration. I uttered in a strong affirmation that had never before ever passed my lips, "If it is within my power, no one - no woman, will ever feel alone again." I thought to myself, if I feel this way, there must be women out there that feel exactly like me. That ARE like me.

In that very moment in time my Inner Warrior emerged. Tapping into my inner self, and becoming engaged in my feminine energy naturally segued to finally surrendering and releasing. To my surprise, it didn't feel like failure at all. As a matter of fact it was, and has been, a series of continuous victories. Why? Because it's a matter of perspective. Little did I know that it was that exact moment that literally changed not only my attitude, but the complete trajectory of my life.

The Passionista

"You don't seek out to be a leader. True leadership finds you."
~Carol Starr Taylor

I have never woken up in the morning and said to myself, "Oh, I think I will be a leader today, I need that for my resume." It's been quite the opposite actually. It has taken a lifetime of being beaten down repeatedly and somehow, to my surprise, getting back up as a new version of myself. You could say I have had more than 'nine lives'.

As the years went on from that fateful day in my car I can say, looking back, that the Universe certainly doesn't work within our timeline. That affirmation and realization did not create an instantaneous 'abracadabra' change in my life. Change within one's self is a process. It's painful for me still, with even more lessons to learn. However, what did change that day was both my belief and perspective. It was as if those tears washed away any remnants of the Shield that still existed — opening the flood gates, by giving myself permission to be my vulnerable, authentic self, and step into my truth.

That metamorphosis has not been an easy one, for sure. However, when I started to live my truth, authenticity, and my passion, the plethora of previous doubts, fears, and anxiety about me and how people viewed me became less and less. Gone is the desire to 'fit in' to the mold. Actually, my quest is to break the ideology of the mold altogether.

Throughout my journey leading to this stage of my life, I have realized that I don't require validation outside of myself to feel lovable. I AM Love. I live with heart and pure love in every fiber of my being. I know that I don't need to be perfect, just real. Life is a symphony of joy, passion, tragedy, experiences, lessons, and magic. It is all in our perception and belief systems as we navigate each day how we view the world, others, and ourselves. The quest for true happiness on the outside is actually not a quest at all, but the Holy Grail found within ourselves is the true treasure.

I have spent the last few years now living my vulnerable and authentic self. I believe that the energy that I have been emitting has attracted magic. It has raised my vibration and the exact vision from that fateful day has now come to fruition. Living my truth and my passion has led me to my ultimate purpose. My Legacy.

Creating, living my legacy, and helping others with their personal imprint on the world have been first and foremost my passions; thus, being a 'Passionista'. The catalyst was the birth of my children and certainly they have remained a significant factor. What hit home even more recently, prompting me to finally write my solo author book, was being a caregiver to my mother who succumbed to her illness at the age of 73. This was not that long ago, and has been a monumental loss for me. After losing both parents, who passed quite young (my father had only been 58 at his time of death), has made me realize that the impact we make with our own lives shouldn't wait.

We have no idea how long we will be here, in this body. Each of us has lived a life of rich lessons to impart on others. Our journey is not to be taken in vain and should be shared. This helps facilitate long lasting change and transformation in others in their personal journey. I have written and gone on stage to talk about my story in order to not only crack open the dialogue, but to reach out to others and let people know that they aren't alone. I have created a global sisterhood, which has now transformed into a safe space for women to share their stories in books, like the one you are reading right now. The power of words is like no other. By establishing a publishing company, it not only allows women who write their stories to experience a cathartic experience, it establishes them as published authors, and also is a catalyst for change to women who read these books all over the world.

One never knows where the roads in their journey will lead. We have all re-evaluated our lives, reframed and reinvented ourselves from time to time - some of us more often than others.

From the voiceless, battered little girl to a Warrior living her passion, truth, purpose and legacy, proves that the magnificence of the human spirit and the Universe has no bounds. Your glorious evolution awaits.

"The whole point of being alive is to evolve into the complete person you were intended to be."
~Oprah Winfrey

Carol Starr Taylor is the Founder of Creative Publishing Group, Writing Coach, Certified Life Coach, NLP Practitioner, International Bestselling Author of the book Life In Pieces— From Chaos to Clarity, Inspirational Speaker, Soulprenuer, and the Founder of The Traveling Sisterhood. She has appeared on TV, Radio, and has been featured in numerous articles. Her passion is to inspire and help facilitate the personal growth of others within themselves and with each other.

Only when we are brave enough
to explore the darkness will we discover
the infinite power of our light.
~ Brene Brown

Teresa Ursini

Landslide

I climbed a mountain, then I turned around and I saw
my reflection in the snow covered hills...
well the landslide BROUGHT ME DOWN."
~Stevie Nicks / Fleetwood Mac

One afternoon standing alone in the drug store while waiting for my thyroid prescription, I stood in front of the sleeping pill aisle, with thoughts racing, "Maybe I could take some sleeping pills and never wake up."

My perfect world had fallen apart. A mother's worst nightmare had become my reality. For many years I was weighed down by my heavy heart, feeling hopeless, as I watched my son spiraling out of control. I felt heartbroken and pained at what he was doing to himself. I was conscious every single day of my daughter having to witness such heartache. As a family, we all watched my son's struggle with drug and alcohol addiction.

I felt like a failure as a mother. Thinking I did everything right, where did it go so wrong? Asking myself the question, did I miss something while my children were growing up? Did I not pay attention to signs along the way, the signs that I thought were that of a normal teenager's behavior? I witnessed such as a huge personality change. He went from a warm, loving, helpful child to a boy who was angry and who would threaten us if we did not give him what he asked for; breaking all the house rules, talking back in a very harsh tone. We had not changed, but he certainly did change to the extreme.

I know now it wasn't him being just a normal teenager but a child/teenager who was experimenting with different drugs, entering into a life of addiction. The drug use had altered his personality, even causing him to hallucinate. He had changed all his friends; I didn't know a single one. I would look in his room and find drawings of devils and demons. I knew this was not going to be an easy road ahead. As a mother I had every right to search his room for signs, to let me know what was going on in his life. He was not talking openly as he once did, but, rather, everything became secretive. I didn't want him doing illegal or harmful things under our roof without my knowledge. I had to find some way, somehow, to get a back bone. I had to become strong and not be his friend, but his voice of reason.

Drug use had changed his sense of reality. He was not able to hold down a job or keep good grades in school. Our eyes were opened, wide and in disbelief, with a situation in twelfth grade. At the end of the year on a day school trip at an amusement park my son had brought a bottle of liquor. He drank pretty much the entire bottle himself. The police were called, and wanted to arrest him for bringing liquor into a public place, and drinking underage.

The police called me at work. I begged them, "Please don't arrest him." They allowed me to take him to the hospital to make sure he did not have alcohol poisoning. It was then discovered he had been engaging in this for a good year; drinking - and drugs. A whole year had passed without me knowing, but now it made sense.

I realized that was why he had such an extreme change in his personality. Right there we knew it was time to get help. I hated the person looking back at me in the mirror. Retreating from everyone and everything, I didn't want to see or feel the pain around me. I tried to harden my heart, so I didn't have to feel. Afraid, and avoiding all socialization for fear that someone would ask those three words, "How are you?" That was all it took to start crying. My husband and I were desperate. We tried to seek help. Where do we even begin? Who do we call for help? We made numerous phone calls to rehab centers, pleading for help with no positive responses.

We wanted to understand and learn more about addiction. Call after call, the same response, "If he doesn't want to get help, then we can't help him - or you." I was determined, and continued to call more rehab centers. Finally on one call the woman on the other end of the phone, hearing the desperation in my voice, said, "Okay, bring your son in on Monday and we will help your family." As I put the phone down, a huge surge of relief filled me. Finally, somebody heard my plea and was willing to help.

My perfect, calm, happy life came to an abrupt standstill. All my hopes and dreams for this life gone, now focusing on this terrible situation, trying to use all the strength I had in my body and mind. It was so hard to tell my son, "You need to go to the rehab center. You will not be allowed to live with us if you don't get help. I will not allow one person to destroy three others living in this house. If we don't take this opportunity now, there might not be another chance for help." After much arguing, he agreed to go.

The same year my son was struggling with his demons, my mother had fallen and severely broken her back causing her to become a paraplegic. That landslide came crashing down hard on me. Those years were the worst years of my life. I had climbed the highest mountain only to come sliding down to the bottom. Most days I found it very hard to get out of bed, feeling so much pain, every minute of the day. At times I just cried uncontrollably. My mind kept going into a dark and lonely place. Where am I going to get the strength to survive these next days and years ahead?

Finding the rehabilitation center where my son would finally get the professional help he needed was comforting. But I knew it was going to be a very long journey ahead. I was grateful to the staff for helping deal with this situation. Three months passed. When my son came home things were looking good, or so I thought. This, as it turned out, was only temporary, as months later he proceeded to relapse. That was the beginning of a terrible yo-yo cycle. Each time he relapsed, it was worse than the last time. Year after year he was in and out of rehab. Year after year I kept feeling worse, more fearful of a future that looked so dark. Feeling like I was on a train, barreling at a very high speed, I was looking straight ahead at a wall, but unable to stop.

My sleep was terrible. I dealt with constant nightmares and having a full night of sleep was impossible. This made handling the trauma even worse. I struggled to function in my day to day life. Trying to take care of everybody was increasingly difficult. I realized I had to make a change for myself and started with finding professional help. Attending a program at the rehab center once a week, along with my husband, for a few years, helped. At the center I learned to use tools to help me deal with a family member suffering with addictions. Listening to other moms sharing the same journey, helpless in watching their loved ones suffer, made it seem that I wasn't alone and was somewhat comforting.

Many days on the drive home all I could think of was, "Please don't let me find my son dead." Opening the door, and then hearing his voice, each time I relaxed a little, knowing we made it one more day. I loved my son so much but I hated what he was doing to himself. Many days I had to fight with him to take a shower and put on clean clothes. He did not care about himself or his personal hygiene. I felt, as his mother, I had to put my own feelings aside and help him by getting tough. I needed to be 'cruel to be kind'. I resented that I had to change my personality to help him but I knew it had to be done. I am not a cruel person. When I say cruel I mean that I learned to not give in to his demands, such as when he would ask me for money. I had to tell him NO!! If he was calling me to pick him up on a cold winter day, I said NO!! He found jobs when he realized he couldn't get money from me, but he still asked me for more. It seemed no matter what I did for him it was never good enough. The doctors all told me not to give him an 'umbrella' to stay dry under. Do not enable him. He seemed to bring out the worst in me. He was not that kind, caring, son I brought into our loving world. I totally lost him to his addiction, and lost part of myself, too.

Rock bottom hit hard when my son disappeared. We drove around the neighborhood the first day, then the second day, and found nothing. As panic started to set in, we called the police and asked for their help. A helicopter search began. He was nowhere to be found. The police officers on bikes looked everywhere, but still nothing. On the third day I received a call from a friend who found him, frightening children and asking for their money, at our local community center. Our friend, who happened to be working that day, recognized him and begged the teacher not to call the police. Instead she would call me. That call was very relieving. But I had no idea what condition I was going to find him in.

As I got into the car to pick him up, my heart started to race faster. Seeing him dirty, thirsty, and hungry, I asked him the question, "Where were you?" His simple answer, "I don't know," truly broke my heart. I called the police to help me bring him to the hospital where his doctor practiced. The nurse told me if we hadn't gotten him to the hospital he might have not been alive by the next day. He was so severely dehydrated and famished. I found out later that afternoon that he had gone on a drug binge without food or fluids for 3 days. Thank goodness the doctor said he was going to keep him in the hospital for as long as it took to get him to detox and onto proper medication.

Asking for help from doctors who specialize in addiction was the first step. Through the rehab center I found an amazing doctor. My son was able to speak openly with him. With the much needed help, education from the rehab center, and with the doctors, my son had his life back on track. I spoke to the doctors myself about my anxiety, which helped deal a little better day to day. The journey ahead was a very long one. There were many twisting, winding roads and forks along the way. Months passed by and things got better. My son took his medication, he had a clearer mind and knew he needed to go back to rehab and get his life on a clean path. Realizing he almost died seemed to change something in him. It took many years of research, in and out of hospitals to get the proper medicine and medical help that my son needed, to move forward to live a productive life. I am very thankful he co-operated in the treatments.

I kept asking myself where I went wrong as a mother. But I needed to stop overthinking everything. It took a long time and much soul searching to realize I was a good mother. I needed to always keep telling myself that. I was a loving mother and I did everything the best I could do. Admitting that I needed to help myself and needed to learn how to let go of a lot of things that I had no control of was healing. I had to learn to go deep into my own honest emotions. I got stronger by listening to music that would soothe my broken heart and soul. I treated myself to the spa occasionally to calm my body and mind. I had to practice keeping myself away from the dark side in my mind. Finally, finding my inner strength by speaking to family and friends, and by being honest about what we were going through, helped. I stopped feeling ashamed that I had a son going through this. It was comforting speaking to people who knew me. It was helpful also speaking with other moms struggling with a child dealing with addiction. No more suffering in silence.

I feel both my son, and our family, are all warriors. We chose to pull together as a family, put our loving arms around him and not let his addictions control us, but rather help him to control his temptations. We held no judgment, only talking about our feelings honestly.

I am the big momma bear who did anything I could to protect my baby cubs. I needed to find some peace and alone time with my own thoughts. I wrote in a journal to process my thoughts, which helped me also. I needed to turn my bad thoughts into more positive ones. I turned a bad situation into a learning life lesson, and to maybe even help others. I wanted to show people not to give up hope. I kept hoping and hoping that one day my life would go back to normal, and that hope kept me going. I spent many years as a volunteer at the rehab center that helped my son. Volunteering my time helping others gave me a heart–warming, rewarding feeling. I was determined not to lose this battle.

My desire to be positive forced me to keep things in my life positive. I had to learn how to forgive my son and to be compassionate. I refused to be angry. I learned how to rebuild my relationship with my son. It was a very hard life lesson which almost killed my spirit; however I decided to push through. I am proud of who I am and I don't try to change myself anymore. I feel at peace that my son is alive, healthy, and holding down a job for many years now.

Proudly and respectfully moving forward, I never want to go through that nightmare again. I have become a stronger person because of the tragedies in my life. I wake up every morning looking forward to a new day and the challenges and blessings it may bring. "Warrior onward."

"I am definitely a stronger person
because of the tribulations in my life.
The good life is one inspired by love,
guided by knowledge."
~Bertrand Russell

Teresa Ursini was born and raised in Toronto, Ontario, Canada. She has been married for 37 years.

A self-employed woman with an entrepreneurial spirit, Teresa is now a #1 International Bestselling Author in the book The Sisterhood Folios Live Out Loud. She enjoys listening to music which has always soothed her soul and has been a source of inspiration and salvation. She lives by the motto "unconditional self-acceptance is the core to a peaceful mind."

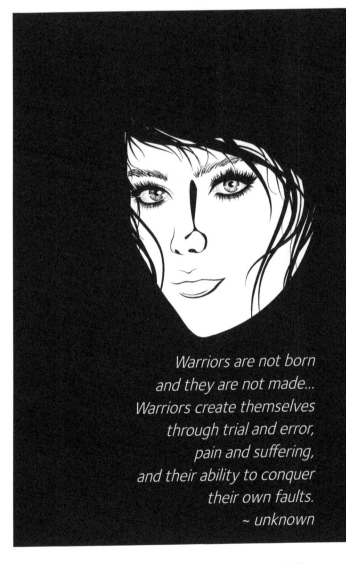

*Warriors are not born
and they are not made...
Warriors create themselves
through trial and error,
pain and suffering,
and their ability to conquer
their own faults.*
~ unknown

CONGRATULATIONS
to all our Authors

We are proud to announce that the first two volumes of The Sisterhood *f*olios have both reached

#1 International Best Seller
status in their categories on Amazon.

Thank you for sharing your stories, enjoy your well earned status.

WHAT IS YOUR STORY?

Have you ever said, "I should write my story"?

Is writing a book on your Bucket List?

Do you realize, that by sharing your journey,
you are helping yourself and others?

Impart your wisdom and make a difference!

This will give you a taste for writing
without the pressure of an entire book!

Are you ready to write your own book?

We also do SOLO AUTHOR projects.

The 4th volume in
The Sisterhood *folios:*

The 5th volume in
The Sisterhood *folios:*

Rebel Rising

F*ck Fear

The first volume in
Women Think Business:

The Balancing Act

Inquire about contributing a chapter.

info@creativepublishinggroup.com
www.creativepublishinggroup.com

CPSIA information can be obtained
at www.ICGtesting.com
Printed in the USA
LVHW02s0306090418
572657LV00006B/8/P

9 781988 820026